# Understanding Cerebral Palsy

## A Guide for Parents and Professionals

### *Marion Stanton*

*Foreword by Joe Whittaker*

Jessica Kingsley *Publishers*
London and Philadelphia

Permission for case studies has been kindly granted by Alan Martin and Dan Stanton.

First published in 2012
by Jessica Kingsley Publishers
116 Pentonville Road
London N1 9JB, UK
and
400 Market Street, Suite 400
Philadelphia, PA 19106, USA

*www.jkp.com*

**Library of Congress Cataloging in Publication Data**
Stanton, Marion, 1956-
  Understanding cerebral palsy : a guide for parents and professionals /
Marion Stanton ; foreword by John Wyatt.
     p. cm. -- (JKP essentials)
  Includes bibliographical references and index.
  ISBN 978-1-84905-060-9 (alk. paper)
 1.  Cerebral palsy. 2.  Developmental disabilities.  I. Title.
  RJ496.C4S86 2012
  618.92'836--dc23
                          2011045664

**British Library Cataloguing in Publication Data**
A CIP catalogue record for this book is available from the British Library

ISBN 978 1 84905 060 9
eISBN 978 0 85700 256 3

Printed and bound in Great Britain

This book is dedicated to Dan Stanton and to the memory of Zahrah Manuel and Christian McLean.

# CONTENTS

# ACKNOWLEDGEMENTS

Thanks to my nephews Andrew Wille and Jonny Shoults for helping me with early drafts.

# FOREWORD

*Understanding Cerebral Palsy* provides a refreshing and systematic appreciation of a condition experienced by people across a wide variety of social contexts. However, unlike other publications this is not simply a medical account of a collection of symptoms related to cerebral palsy, but a book that very quickly contextualizes the unique ways in which the individual may experience and manage *their* cerebral palsy to live *their* life with support they consider effective.

The underpinning values of this book are based upon the importance of meaningful relationships, informed by the social model of disability, which is described and applied throughout. The social model of disability does not present the individual with CP as a 'problem' to be solved or as a 'burden' to be overcome but generates an understanding, away from an individual's impairments, and a carefully detailed analysis of the ways society can be changed to meet the support requirements of the individual with CP. Such a social model approach to any impairment is likely to promote and enhance human rights and dignity of the individual, where the individual is not defined by impairment but a society's value and worth can judged by its response to that individual.

Marion illustrates in many ways how relationships between a person with CP and professionals can be highly productive when collaboration is an integral objective. A professional can have a great deal of knowledge about cerebral palsy, which can include minute and extensive details relating to the physiology of a person with CP, the genetic composition and causation of CP, and the skills to analyze a whole range of statistical data relating to groups of people with CP, and yet with all these skills and knowledge the professional can know nothing about Daniel, who happens to experience CP, without having a meaningful relationship with Daniel. Such a relationship is unlikely to succeed without a mutually accessible communication system, as a way of cementing crucial understandings between two human beings.

There is a useful historical context that locates current disability issues into a wider political context, highlighting the significant shifts and benchmarks over the centuries. It traces the history from the time when segregating disabled people was a default position within society, to a place where disabled people are taking control over the direction of their lives and the supports they receive to live that life. This approach is becoming increasingly significant as disabled people have to engage with the myriad of assumptions used by professional bodies who are charged with the processing of disabled people through 'assessment' 'measurement' and 'treatment' often without specific consent from the individual being processed.

Marion does not avoid controversial issues, which may be related to the pros and cons of particular therapies or the personal decisions about vaccinations and the management of continence for instance. The book also acknowledges that people with cerebral palsy have a sexuality and will go on to lead sexually active lives, a view which may still cause consternation to many of the statutory and voluntary services who have established organizations and charities to manage the lives of people with cerebral palsy.

The book devotes a whole chapter to 'Alternatives to Verbal Communication' (Chapter 6). It offers practical solutions to complex communication issues — Marion has systematically stripped down the rhetoric and professional jargon to reveal the essential elements of good communication between the individual with CP and the professional, where a head or eye movement or a pointing gesture can be the start of beautiful relationship.

Marion introduces the reader to the labyrinth of the world of voluntary and statutory services that have evolved to 'support' people with CP but she deftly shows how services can be transformed to effective support service when they take their cues from the individual who is living with CP. The notion of 'support' is critically analyzed, where support can only meaningfully be called support if it matches the individual's particular requirements rather than what 'others' decide his or her 'support' should be.

This is an optimistic description of how environments can be changed to enhance the richness of a person's contribution to all aspects of society regardless of a particular impairment. The reader is presented with a set of questions about meaningful experiences from individual living with CP; it offers a range of valuable exercises to guide the reader to a more informed position where further understanding and constructive judgment can be made.

Integral to the fabric of this book is the 'voice' of the person living with cerebral palsy, a voice that must be heard if we are to change the world for the better, where we can all be enriched by our mutual interests.

*Joe Whittaker*
*Chair of The Alliance for Inclusive Education*

Chapter 1

# AN INTRODUCTION TO CEREBRAL PALSY

No two people who have cerebral palsy will be the same. Cerebral palsy (or CP as it is often referred to) can affect those who have it very mildly so that you would hardly notice they had an impairment. It can be moderate, in which case you would be likely to notice the unsteady movements or stiffness of limb but the person who has the CP would still be able to go about his daily life with minimal help. It can be very severe so that the person is unable to move at all. There are many shades in between these three presentations of CP. This variability makes learning about the condition, diagnosing the condition, treating the condition and making outcome predictions extremely difficult.

Cerebral palsy affects children, often from birth, and persists for life. One of the most difficult aspects of CP is that it is hard to know in a child's early years whether he will grow up with mild, moderate or severe cerebral palsy. The extent of his disability unfolds as he grows. These factors contribute enormously to the confusion and frustration often felt by carers who are trying to do their best to give their child a positive start in life.

## WHAT IS CEREBRAL PALSY?

Cerebral palsy is *a disorder of movement*. The term relates to the physical condition of a person who has difficulty either producing movement, preventing movement or controlling movement following injury to the brain before or during birth or in the first five years of life. The physical problems presented by cerebral palsy are often referred to as *motor* problems.

A child with CP may also have additional disabilities, caused by damage to parts of the brain other than those controlling motor function, such as visual or hearing problems, other sensory problems, perceptual difficulties or language delay.

There is no cure for cerebral palsy. Damaged brain cells cannot regenerate. However, many believe that there are ways in which the effects of brain damage may be brought under control so that the individual can live a more fulfilling life than might otherwise have been the case.

Doctors can be reluctant to diagnose cerebral palsy when a child is showing signs which lead them to suspect it. There may be a number of reasons for this:

- It is not always easy to identify (especially in the very young baby) and doctors are wary of misinforming parents.

- Even when a child has clearly sustained damage to the brain or starts to show signs of having cerebral palsy, there are numerous instances of symptoms disappearing leaving the child free of any motor problems or other impairments.

- There are wide variations in the severity of the condition so parents may misinterpret minor problems as being very severe.

- Doctors may exercise caution in informing parents of their suspicions because they fear that the parent will be unable to cope with the information.

- Early symptoms of CP might give way to other problems which are more of an issue than the motor problems.

## WHAT CAUSES CEREBRAL PALSY?

The brain damage may be due to one of a number of factors. Up to 50 per cent of cases of CP have no known cause at present. The following are some of the most common known causes.

### Prenatal causes (before birth)

HAEMORRHAGE

Haemorrhage (bleeding) in a specific area of the brain is a common cause with premature children who develop cerebral palsy.

INFECTION

Infection may be passed from mother to child in the womb. An example of this is the passing on of cytomegalo-virus (CMV) to the unborn child.

The virus is a harmless member of the herpes family but can (in a very small number of cases) cause brain damage to a child if passed to him during pregnancy. German measles (rubella) is a more commonly known virus which can be passed to the child in the womb and cause brain damage.

ENVIRONMENTAL FACTORS

Environmental factors mean that the mother can be affected by something she eats or drinks, or by breathing dangerous poisons in the air, which can be passed on to the child before birth. Toxoplasmosis is an infection which may be acquired from eating raw or undercooked meat, from cats or from contact with contaminated soil. The infection can then be passed on to the unborn child. Radiation received by the mother (e.g. through radiotherapy) can also affect the unborn child. There have been a number of specific incidents where the number of children affected in certain geographical areas increased temporarily due to environmental pollution. An epidemic of CP occurred in Minamata Bay, Japan, between 1953 and 1971. This was eventually found to be related to methyl mercury in fish which had been consumed by pregnant women. The discharge of methyl mercury had come from a vinyl chloride acetaldehyde plant (Kondo 2000).

HEREDITY

There has been speculation that a small number of cases may be hereditary (Schaefer 2008).

## Perinatal causes (at or around the time of birth: 28 weeks of pregnancy to around one month after birth)

LACK OF OXYGEN TO THE BRAIN (ASPHYXIA)

Lack of oxygen is a common cause in cases where there are difficulties at birth, such as the umbilical cord being wrapped round the child's neck, the mother haemorrhaging before the baby has been safely delivered, or contractions which are so severe that the supply of oxygen from the placenta is reduced.

## Postnatal cause (in the first five years of life)

HEAD INJURY

Head injuries sustained during the first five years of life may cause CP.

INFECTION

Infections such as meningitis contracted in early life can cause CP.

LACK OF OXYGEN

CP can be caused by the brain being deprived of oxygen for a period of time due to accident or choking during the first five years of life. A near-miss cot death or a near-drowning inhalation can have the same effect.

## DIFFERENT TYPES OF CP

The way in which a child's movement is affected will depend on the extent of the brain damaged and which areas of the brain are damaged. This is because specific areas of the brain control different motor functions. There are four main 'types' of cerebral palsy. These are spastic, athetoid, ataxic and mixed.

### Spastic cerebral palsy (pyramidal)

Spastic CP is caused by damage to the cortex. The child will be stiff in one or more limbs and possibly all over.

### Athetoid cerebral palsy (extra-pyramidal)

Athetoid CP is caused by damage to the basal ganglia and/or cerebellum (see Figure 1.1). The child may be floppy in one or more limbs, possibly all over whilst many may have high or fluctuating tone with accompanying constant uncontrolled movements.

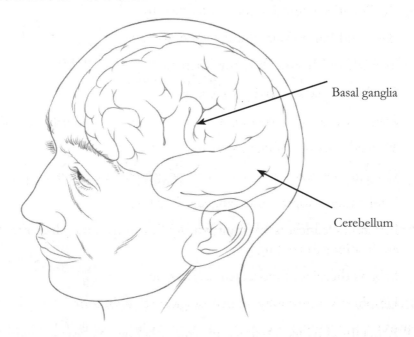

Basal ganglia

Cerebellum

*Figure 1.1 Figure of the brain showing the site of damage for different types of CP.*
*Courtesy of: Patrick J. Lynch, medical illustrator; C. Carl Jaffe, MD, cardiologist.*

## Ataxic cerebral palsy

Ataxic CP is caused by damage to the cerebellum (see Figure 1.1). The child will be unsteady. Although movement is present it may appear random and bringing these random movements under control may be difficult.

## Mixed cerebral palsy

Mixed CP is a term used for types of cerebral palsy which do not fit neatly into one of the other three classifications. The child may show signs of more than one type of cerebral palsy.

## Other types of cerebral palsy

Other, less common, types of cerebral palsy include *dystonia*, where posture distorts intermittently; it can sometimes be present with other types of CP (e.g. a child may have athetoid CP and also have dystonia), *chorea*, where fingers and toes jerk spontaneously, *ballismus*, where there is uncontrolled movement of the joints, *rigidity*, where limbs are rigid like lead piping or intermittently resist passive motion, *tremor* and *atonia*, which is similar to athetosis and often develops into it.

## Topographical classification

Cerebral palsy is most commonly classified topographically (in terms of the parts of the body affected and the extent of the disability), as detailed below.

QUADRIPLEGIA

All four limbs are affected.

DIPLEGIA

All four limbs are affected but the legs more so than the arms. This is common if CP occurs due to a premature birth.

PARAPLEGIA

Both legs are affected.

TRIPLEGIA

Three limbs are affected.

HEMIPLEGIA

One side of the body is affected. This is a type of CP that can be the result of a bleed on the brain prior to birth.

MONOPLEGIA

One limb is affected.

## Other common factors

Additional disabilities may be fairly common (due to damage to areas of the brain other than those relating to motor function) and include such problems as difficulty in developing speech, difficulty in seeing or difficulty making sense of what is seen, difficulty in hearing or difficulty making sense of what is heard, having either mild or severe seizures (convulsions or fits), and learning difficulties. Later on there may be difficulty with organizing the written word (e.g. dyslexia). It is common to find difficulty with reading and spelling among otherwise cognitively able children who have CP (Sandberg 2006). There is a danger – in certain more severe cases – of muscle contracture (muscles stretching out of shape) and resultant bone deformities. Speech delay could be a result of motor impairment of the muscles which control the movement of the tongue and lips essential for speech and is not necessarily a reflection of a child's intellectual abilities.

## Additional terminology

Confusion often arises for parents when doctors offer a different diagnosis or use terms which are not immediately identifiable with a known condition. The following terms (in addition to cerebral palsy and sometimes instead of the term) might be used. Some children who do not have cerebral palsy might present with the following problems and some children who have cerebral palsy also appear to present with one or more of the following conditions.

MOTOR DELAY

Motor delay means that the child is behind the average in developing normal movement in limbs and body. This will be assessed by noting where a child fails to achieve a 'motor milestone' – such as sitting up by six months or walking by 12–18 months.

DEVELOPMENTAL DELAY

Developmental delay means that the child is behind the average in her motor, vision and fine speech, language and social development.

GLOBAL DELAY

Global delay has a similar meaning to developmental delay but tends to be used where a consultant believes that all aspects of a child's development are affected.

INTELLECTUAL IMPAIRMENT

Intellectual impairment means that the consultant believes the child's understanding is affected, to an extent which will cause learning difficulties.

SENSORY IMPAIRMENT

Sensory impairment means that one or more of the child's senses – touch, taste, sight, hearing and smell – are affected. There are other sensory areas, such as proprioception (the ability to have a sense of yourself in space) and the vestibular system (affecting balance), which might also be affected.

CORTICAL BLINDNESS OR CORTICAL VISUAL IMPAIRMENT

Cortical blindness is caused by damage to the cerebral cortex. This means that the child has difficulty making sense of what he sees but it does not necessarily mean that he is blind in the conventional sense. He may be clinically able to see but unable to organize what he sees. There is evidence that sight can improve with visual stimulation.

MULTIPLE HANDICAPS

Multiply handicapped is a general term for children who have several problems of which cerebral palsy may be one.

EPILEPSY

Epilepsy is used to describe fits or seizures caused by sudden electrical activity in the brain.

## CLASSIFICATION OF CEREBRAL PALSY

The following classification of cerebral palsy is based on the work of Minear (1956).

### Physiological

Physiological classification refers to description by type of movements.

1.  Spasticity (stiff)
2.  Athetosis (floppy):
    a.  tensional (sometimes tense)
    b.  non-tensional (not tense)
    c.  dystonic (muscles lack strength)
    d.  with tremor (muscles quiver)
3.  Rigidity (stiff or no movement)
4.  Ataxia (movements irregular and jerky)
5.  Tremor
6.  Atonia (rare; muscles lack vigour)
7.  Mixed (combination of some or all of above)
8.  Unclassifiable

## Topographical

Topographical classification refers to the parts of the body that are affected.

1.  Monoplegia: affects one limb
2.  Paraplegia: affects only the legs
3.  Hemiplegia: affects one side of the body
4.  Triplegia: affects three limbs
5.  Quadriplegia (tetraplegia): affects all four limbs
6.  Diplegia: affecting both halves uniformly: bilaterial paralysis

## Double hemiplegia: affecting all four limbs but arms more so than legs. Aetiological

Aetiological classification refers to different possible causes.

1.  Prenatal (before birth):
    a.  hereditary-genetic
    b.  acquired in the womb:
        i.   infection
        ii.  anoxia (lack of oxygen)

    iii.  prenatal cerebral haemorrhage

    iv.  Rhesus factor

    v.  metabolic: inability to adapt nutrition to service bodily function needs

    vi.  breech delivery

    vii.  poor maternal nutrition

2.  Natal (at birth)

    a.  Anoxia:

        i.  placental failure

        ii.  drug induced

        iii.  breech delivery

        iv.  forceps delivery

        v.  maternal anoxia or hypotension

3.  Postnatal (after birth)

    a.  accident

    b.  infection

    c.  poisoning

    d.  blood vessel damage

    e.  anoxia

    f.  tumour

## Incidental factors

Incidental factors include other, non-motor, problems which might arise.

1.  Intellectual impairment

2.  Physical state:

    a.  small size of body

    b.  developmental delay

    c.  poor bone development

    d.  contractures: permanent distortion of muscles

3.  Eye and hand movement

4.  Vision:

    a.  sensory loss; damaged cortical area of the brain

    b.  motor; control of eye movement or direction affected by poor muscle control

5.  Hearing:

    a.  loss of pitch

    b.  loss of decibels

6.  Speech disorders

7.  Touch:

    a.  oversensitive

    b.  not sensitive

8.  Taste and smell:

    a.  oversensitive

    b.  not sensitive

9.  Convulsions

10. In 2005 Bax *et al.* proposed a new way of classifying CP noting that previous classification systems such as Minear's were focussed exclusively on motor deficit. They proposed an updated definition of CP that recognised CP as a group of motor disorders which 'may be accompanied by disturbance of sensation, cognition, communication, perception, and/or behaviour, and/or by a seizure disorder.' The authors argued that, in addition to describing CP, predictive issues to inform future health care should also be taken into account as well as case comparison and evaluation of change within individuals (Bax *et al.* 2005).


## ADDITIONAL QUESTIONS REGARDING CEREBRAL PALSY

### Is intelligence affected?

Many carers of children who have cerebral palsy fear that their child may not be intelligent. Intelligence is very complicated and clinical understanding of intelligence is still developing.

The assessment of a child's understanding is very difficult when they are young. Tests designed to assess intelligence often require children to have full use of their hands, good hearing and good vision – and may therefore not be appropriate for testing a child who has cerebral palsy. To counter this, therapists will also observe the child's responses to everyday situations. However, these are very difficult to interpret if a child has a problem controlling his movement. Physical disability may inhibit the child's ability to express his mental alertness. In addition to this, assumptions made that a young child is intellectually impaired may lead to his not receiving the appropriate stimulation for his age. This, in turn, could lead to the child failing to develop intellectually to his full capacity but it would be social and environmental factors which were to blame, not the brain damage. This is particularly a problem for non-speaking children. There is still a common view that if you can't speak, it reflects an inability to understand. Nothing could be further from the truth but it is a position that is difficult to shift in a world where so much relies on spoken language. Thankfully, new technology, with the emergence of communication aids with electronic voices, is offering new possibilities to those who cannot speak.

Until a child develops a clear means of communication, it is impossible to tell whether they have intellectual impairment. Some children who have cerebral palsy will develop speech at the same rate as a non-disabled child. In the event that speech is delayed, the safest course of action is to offer the same opportunities that you would to a speaking child. The family may see a sign that a child understands before consultants or therapists do. Professionals may believe that parents overestimate their children's intellectual capabilities because of a strong desire to believe that their children understand. A psychologist and/or speech and language therapist may be asked to assess your child's intellectual capacities. It will be helpful if these professionals have understanding of the ways in which non-speaking children who have normal intellectual ability can be helped through AAC strategies. It is a good idea for parents to keep records of their children's achievements to share with professionals. Video can be very useful for this.

Beliefs about intelligence and the way in which the intelligence is affected in children who have CP have changed over the past 100 years. In 1889 Sir William Osler asserted that children with bilateral hemiplegia (now known as spastic quadriplegia) were usually 'imbecile and often idiotic', children with paraplegia offered 'greater hope of mental improvement', a large percentage of children with hemiplegia grew up to be 'feeble minded' and that epilepsy was a 'potent factor in inducing mental deterioration' (Osler and Baird 1991).

In the 1940s, Dr Phelps maintained that 30 per cent of persons with cerebral palsy were 'mentally defective' and 70 per cent were 'normal'

(Phelps 1948). Other publications tended to quote the incidence of 'mental deficiency' at around 50 per cent. In the 1950s, Crothers and Paine (1959) suggested that the incidence of 'mental deficiency' varied from one category to another of the condition. They maintained that of 80 per cent of 'spastics' with three or more limbs involved, 60 per cent of hemiplegias and 50 per cent of extra-pyramidal cases had an IQ below average (Crothers and Paine 1959).

In the 1970s, Sophie Levitt reported that intelligence varied among 'spastics', tending to be lower than in 'athetoids', was frequently good and may be very high in 'athetoids', and was often low in cases of ataxia (Levitt 1977).

The language we use to describe cognitive ability has changed over the years. Terms like 'mental defective' and 'retardation' are no longer considered acceptable.

The reality is that no one can predict the cognitive development of a child who has CP with certainty. However, incorrect assumptions could lead to frustrated children failing to express their real abilities. It is more useful to look at ways of maximizing a child's learning.

Over recent years there has been a shift of emphasis away from the assumption that intelligence is determined by the extent and type of brain damage and towards a more complex analysis of the development of the intelligence in which many factors play a part. Environmental factors are now considered to make a significant contribution to the development of intelligence. In the 1940s, Hebb (1949) maintained that intellectual performance depended on 'cell assembly' developed through repeated stimulation. The notion of the importance of a stimulating environment began to have some prominence (Hebb 1949).

In the 1970s, Rosenbaum outlined four different pathways along which children make developmental progress. These are:

- physical
- intellectual
- emotional
- social.

They considered that motor (movement) behaviour acts as a linking and integrating mechanism in development. They proposed that there is a relationship between movement and aspects of intellectual development. They also suggested that motor behaviour contributes to emotional and social development and pointed out that frustration, dependence and lack of social interaction suffered by a child with cerebral palsy increases the likelihood of emotional disturbance and psychiatric disorder. They proposed that programmes should be devised to ensure that children gain motor experience which is aimed at promoting overall development rather than being special to a child's physical difficulties (Rosenbaum, Barnitt and Brand 1975).

In 1997 a group of Japanese researchers found that the IQ levels of a group of children with CP varied according to the type of elementary education they had received (Ito *et al.* 1997).

Schmidt and Vojens (2003) found that there are often four specific areas of cognitive deficit in some children who have CP while the rest of cognition may remain intact. These are:

- concentration

- the ability to combine and structure situations or data

- completing a task or sequence

- short-term memory.

Schmidt and Vojens (2003) also contend that traditional IQ tests fail to establish the cognitive status of children who have CP.

Several studies have found that up to 50 per cent of children with CP who have normal intelligence have difficulty with literacy (Glennen and DeCoste 1997, p.285). There may be a number of factors which explain this, including:

- additional damage to the area of the brain that supports the learning of literacy

- lack of opportunity for graphic practice (writing)

- lack of opportunity for phonic practice (using voice to practise the sounds of letter groups)

- difficulty with tracking (following the lines on the page) due to movement difficulty.

There is advice in regard to teaching literacy in Chapter 10 on 'Education'.

It appears, therefore, that our intellectual abilities are affected by many inputs and it may be inferred that it is not possible to predict or assume intelligence levels in children who have cerebral palsy as the acquisition of intelligence is determined by many factors external to the child.

Some children with CP do appear to have learning difficulties but this is not necessarily related to the degree of physical disability. Having a learning difficulty does not take away your personality and individuality. Parents may fear this because of the common attitude in society that those who have learning difficulties are less whole than those who do not. There is no optimum level of knowledge and understanding. Every individual, with or without a disability, will be different in how and what they know and perceive. I have met many people who have been labelled as having learning difficulties who have a perception of the world and of themselves which I admire and aspire to. I have also met many people without learning difficulties that I do not.

The basal ganglia and the cerebellum are two areas of the brain that are primarily responsible for motor control (movement). Where cerebral palsy occurs only in these areas, there is a presumption that cognitive function is not affected. However, it is possible that damage to the basal ganglia (which occurs in athetoid cerebral palsy but may also be present in other types of cerebral palsy) may also cause some personality difficulties. This might include rigidity of thought or obsessive behaviour (Joseph 2000). Later research also suggests that high order cognitive functions may be affected by damage to the basal ganglia (Koziol and Budding 2009). Damage to the cerebellum may have an effect on emotional expression resulting in extreme or inappropriate emotional reactions (Turner *et al.* 2007).

Problems with speech frequently occur in children who have CP. It is more common in the population of children who have athetoid cerebral palsy and those children who have more severe motor impairments. Difficulty with speech is often associated with general motor problems with the result that the muscles in the mouth that are used for speech are impaired. This is known as oral dyspraxia. Communication ability does not associate with the ability to understand language. Many children who do not speak understand language. AAC support is essential for this group of children, ideally from the youngest possible age. There is more information about AAC in Chapter 6 on 'Alternatives to Verbal Communication'.

## Can cerebral palsy get worse as the child gets older?

A part of the brain has been irreparably damaged but the damage will not get any worse unless the child suffers further damage following a separate incident. It is possible in many instances for children who have cerebral palsy to gain increasingly greater control over their movement. This may be due to treatment, determination on the part of the child, partial recovery of the brain or just something inexplicable. In some cases the child will appear to recover totally. Total recovery is likely to happen only where the symptoms are not too severe and will take place very early on in the child's life, usually in the first year. A study done by Nelson and Ellenberg (1982) showed that only 111 of 229 children who were suspected to have cerebral palsy under the age of one year went on to develop cerebral palsy by the age of seven. There are a number of theories as to why this happens. Some theorists believe that where damage is not too severe the still developing brain can take compensatory measures, or, more simply, another part of the brain takes over the function of the damaged area. The damage is still present in the brain but the child's ability to function is restored. This is known as neuroplasticity (MemoryZine 2010).

It is also possible for a child to seem to have less control over his movement as time goes on. This is likely to be due to the fact that the effect of the brain damage becomes more apparent as the child gets older rather than to any deterioration in the child's condition. Very rarely cysts on the brain may cause excessive fluid to build up on the brain (hydrocephalus), the pressure of which can cause brain damage. This condition can be relieved by medical treatment or an operation.

## STATISTICS ON INCIDENCE AND PREVALENCE

- *Incidence* refers to the number of new cases occurring during a certain time period in a particular population considered to be at risk – for example, the number of cases per 1000 premature births.

- *Prevalence* refers to the number of cases occurring during a certain time period in an overall population, for example, the number of cases per 1000 live births.

Despite improved obstetric care it has been noted that there was no significant change in the prevalence of cerebral palsy among children born in the North of England between 1960 and 1976. The range of severity has not been noted to change over time either. It has been suggested that this could be due to the fact that more sophisticated methods of resuscitation are now leading to the survival of children who, in the early 2000s, would have died, at the same time as enabling others, who would have just survived with severe disability, to now present with more mild disabilities as treatment techniques continue to improve. The total prevalence of cerebral palsy is generally reckoned to be 2 per 1000 live births (0.2%).

Research in the Netherlands on the prevalence of cerebral palsy and how it changed between 1977 and 1988 found that the average prevalence was 1.51 per 1000 inhabitants. It also found that the prevalence rose over time changing from 0.77 per 1000 between 1977 and 1979 to 2.44 per 1000 between 1986 and 1988 (Johnson 2002).

Ann Johnson studied prevalence in 13 geographic areas in Europe from 1980 to 1990. She found the average to be 2.08 per 1000 live births over the period (Johnson 2002).

Researchers in Atlanta found a slight increase in the prevalence of congenital CP (i.e. present at birth). The rise was from 1.7 to 2.0 per 1000 live births between 1975 and 1991 (Johnson 2002).

A study in China found that the prevalence of CP in those less than seven years old was 1.6 per thousand in 1997 (Liu *et al.* 1999). This study also found that the prevalence in the low birth weight group was higher in China than in developed countries and that more of the low birth weight children died in China than did in developed countries (Liu *et al.* 1999).

In 2008 a study of children with CP in the Asian community in Yorkshire in the UK found a higher prevalence than the national norm being 3.87 to 4.16 per 1000 (Sinha *et al.* 1997). There was a suggestion that this supports the theory that CP may have a genetic aspect within the Asian community studied. In general no difference in prevalence is found in developing or developed countries (Clark and Hankins 2003).

A study in northern Alberta found that there was a trend of increased survival rates for children with CP who had been born very pre-term between 2001 and 2003 in contrast to a decrease between 1993 and 1994 (Robertson, Watt and Yasui 2007). This reversal of trend could well be due to the better standards of care and more sophisticated techniques that have become available.

When severe asphyxia occurs in infants born at term (after a pregnancy of 37 weeks or more), it is generally found that severe spastic quadriplegia is the most common result with a small number of children presenting with athetosis. Asphyxia in pre-term infants is more likely to result in spastic diplegia and minimal other handicap. Contrary to earlier popular belief, it has been found that asphyxia at birth is not a major cause of cerebral palsy. In one study only 8 per cent of cases in Western Australia born between 1975 and 1980 were known to have this cause (Blair and Stanley 2007). In many of the other cases the damage will either have occurred earlier or will be sustained some time after the baby has been born.

It is thought that approximately 70–80 per cent of children with cerebral palsy have the spastic type of CP, 10–20 per cent have athetoid CP, and 5–10 per cent have ataxic CP (Origins of Cerebral Palsy (n.d.)).

Cerebral palsy is a varied condition. I hope that this book will equip you with the information you need to make decisions to help ensure that your child gets maximum opportunities to enjoy a full life, whatever his condition.

# Chapter 2

# SHOULD THERAPY AND TREATMENT BE YOUR FIRST PRIORITY?

A disabled child has the right to enjoy a full and decent life, in conditions which ensure dignity, promote self-reliance, and facilitate the child's active participation in the community. (UN Convention on the Rights of the Child 1989)

The type and amount of therapy and treatment that families are offered will vary depending on the area they live in. They have the choice to say 'Yes' or 'No' to what they are offered and to seek alternative forms of support from other geographical areas as well as from the private sector (although the latter almost always costs money and this may pose problems). There are instances where local service providers may feel strongly enough about an intervention that they seek legal protective custody so that they can insist on the intervention being carried out, but this is not common.

## AN EXERCISE FOR PARENTS AND CARERS

Before I describe various medical and therapeutic techniques I would like you to consider your child's needs in relation to the world he is going to grow up in. This is probably going to affect his ability to develop and grow just as much, and with equally far-reaching implications, as the amount of physiotherapy and other therapy he receives.

Begin by considering the following statements and mark whether you strongly agree, agree, disagree or strongly disagree.

| Statement | Strongly agree | Agree | Disagree | Strongly disagree |
|---|---|---|---|---|
| I want my child to enjoy life | | | | |
| I want my child to have lots of friends | | | | |
| I want my child to be able to make choices | | | | |
| I want my child to go to an ordinary school | | | | |
| I want my child to walk | | | | |
| I want my child to talk | | | | |
| I want my child to be able to use his hands | | | | |
| I want my child to see | | | | |
| I want my child to hear | | | | |
| I want my child to lead a normal life | | | | |
| I want my child to be intelligent | | | | |
| If my child does not learn to walk he will not be a happy person | | | | |
| If my child does not learn to walk I will not be a happy person | | | | |
| People with disabilities must try to fit in with society | | | | |
| Society should be able to include people with disabilities so that their needs can be met more easily | | | | |
| There is nothing a person with a disability cannot do with the right support | | | | |

When you have marked the statements, think about why you marked them as you did. Are you feeling that your child must become as near 'normal' as possible? Do you feel that this is the only way he can live a fulfilled life? Do you feel that there is something wrong with your child? Have you considered his social and friendship needs as well as his need to perform everyday activities such as walking and talking? Do you feel that he will only have a full social life if he walks and talks? Are you concerned that he should get 'better'? Do you feel that the whole thing is too big for you to handle? Would you prefer to entrust your child's development to 'professionals'? Do you distrust the professionals and feel that you should go all out to find a better way to help your child? Do you feel that therapy and treatment is a waste of time and that it is more important to enable your child to be accepted for who he is as he is? Are you afraid that your child will not live up to your expectations? Are you afraid that you will not be able to live up to your own expectations as carer of your child?

Many of these questions could be asked of the parent of a child without a disability. The difference is that your situation is less predictable with a few extra problems tagged on. A lot of expectations tend to get placed on people with disabilities in order that they will fit in better to a non-disabled world. We are all conditioned to expect certain behaviour and abilities from our children and our expectations are based on our knowledge of what is considered 'normal' in the social circle and environment we live in. If our children are not able to fulfil our expectations, not only are we likely to panic but also so are those around us. How well your child is able to integrate into society and live a full life within it is likely to be heavily influenced by your attitude towards him in his early years. Your attitude will influence the attitudes of others he comes into contact with. These attitudes will in turn affect his confidence and ability to take his place in the world.

## HISTORICAL CONTEXT

Disability has been seen differently at various points in history. The Greeks used to kill children who were born with a disability as they were regarded either as economic burdens who served no useful purpose or as retribution from the gods. In the 18th century in Britain 'cripples' were considered to be lower class citizens along with beggars, unemployed people and those who had fallen from grace through vice. In the late 18th century institutions started to spring up to which people with disabilities could be removed. These were not places of care and treatment but places where those considered a burden and an embarrassment could be kept away from ordinary life, where their bodily needs would be met without disruption to society.

In the 1970's, some states in the USA were still carrying out compulsory sterilization of people considered to be mentally handicapped. The last sterilization in the USA took place in 1981 (http://civilliberty.about.com/od/gendersexuality/tp/Forced-Sterilization-History.htm, accessed 17th December 2011).

In the 18th century there was a fairly successful move in the deaf community to promote communication by signing. However, under the influence of a school of thought inspired by Charles Darwin, which held that 'defectives' were unnatural and every measure should be taken to eradicate disability, attempts were made to ban signing and to stop deaf people from marrying each other in case it led to the human race becoming deaf. This suppression is still having its effect today with strong debate still carrying on between those professionals who support signing and those who feel that deaf people must learn to speak in order to fit into society. This is even though there is strong evidence that children who are not allowed to sign are less likely to achieve academically, and are more vulnerable to child abuse, because they have had their means of early communication taken away from them. There are many deaf people today who can remember having their hands tied behind their backs in school in an attempt to force them to communicate orally.

## THE POSITION OF PEOPLE WITH DISABILITIES TODAY

A more 'humane' approach has recently developed (alongside advances in technology) which involves every attempt being made to render the child as near to non-disabled as possible with the use of drugs, surgery and therapy. The emphasis remains on creating as little obvious sign of disability in public as possible. This approach still sees the impairment as a problem that needs fixing.

There is a powerful disability rights lobby led by adults with disabilities who argue for a normal life before a life that is dominated by therapies which aim to lessen the disabled child's impairments. The main focus of the movement is to argue for equal rights for those who have disabilities. The movement does not necessarily object to treatment and therapy but the emphasis is on persuading the local community and society at large that people with disabilities can be accommodated and make a positive contribution as they are.

I encountered this movement very early in my own son's life and I have found that engagement with adults who have CP (and other disabilities) and who are able to articulate their feelings about intervention has been very helpful to me both as a parent of a child with CP who has difficulty with communication and as a practitioner offering interventions. See the Useful Addresses and Contacts section to contact these groups.

People with impairments have been treated very differently throughout history and across different perspectives. The medical model of disability is the most common viewpoint held today. The main thrust of this view is that people with disabilities should be 'treated', 'changed', 'improved' and made more 'normal'. The medical view looks at the problems which children with disabilities are seen to have and applies therapeutic, medical and special teaching techniques in order that they will be better able to fit into the world as it stands.

The disability rights movement views the needs of children who have disabilities in terms of the social world they live in. They look around at the environment and suggest changes which could be made to it to better enable people with disabilities to enjoy full and active lives. This is known as the social model of disability. We don't have to look far before we come up against barriers to progress: ill-equipped mainstream schools and workplaces, lack of adequate training for teachers and employers, funding geared towards treatments rather than adaptations in the environment, ignorance and fear on the part of the majority of the population, which drives carers of children with disabilities indoors to hide their children from cruel stares and remarks. The main focus of the disability rights movement is to ensure that people with disabilities have as much of a say in the running of society as any other citizen. Another focus, pioneered by a strong parent lobby that has been influenced by the disability rights movement, has involved the provision of services that prioritizes the choice of the person with a disability in determining how they will live their life.

There are numerous organizations which have been set up to provide information and practical help for people who have disabilities. Most of these organizations are run for people with disabilities rather than by them. Some make every effort to get people with disabilities on to the committee of management but, in the main, organizations which set out to improve the quality of life for people with disabilities are organized and controlled by non-disabled people. There is some change happening and more organizations run by people with disabilities are developing to tackle specific and general issues (see Useful Addresses and Contacts section).

## CONSIDERATIONS FOR PARENTS AND CARERS

While you are considering what steps to take to help your child, it is always worth asking the question: 'For whose benefit?' I'm not suggesting that children with cerebral palsy should not receive treatment or that they should not be given every opportunity to develop educationally. All children need assistance to develop and flourish and a child with disabilities is no exception. They may even require some extra input to enable them to develop. I am, however, asking you to consider which steps are necessary for your child's well-being and which might be more concerned with normalization or making care easier to manage rather than having a direct benefit to the child.

The problems begin with the lack of day to day contact between disabled and non-disabled people. Research has shown that up to 88 per cent of non-disabled people are not in regular contact with a person who has a physical disability. To answer the question of why there is such a lack of contact we need to examine the opportunity for contact. For many children this begins as soon as they are recognized as having a visible disability. Some common reasons why parents don't take their disabled children out include:

- a desire to protect the child from physical and emotional harm

- embarrassment about the child's disability

- sheer difficulty getting out and about with the child.

Another factor which may influence the early segregation of children comes from medical and educational establishments. A significant amount of the child's time can be taken up in visits to specialists, hospital admissions, medical and psychological assessments, physiotherapy and administration of drugs. A host of well-meaning interventions can combine to take up almost the whole of a child's waking existence. This can lead to isolation, not only of the child, but also of the carer. Also, the scene is set in which the child is perceived as 'different', first and foremost, with the emphasis being on the child having to work towards eliminating this difference. Yet this very aim is sometimes contradicted by the unusual environment which the treatment situation often constructs for children who have disabilities. Therapy should *complement* normal life, not replace it.

Can you imagine how you yourself could have developed into a normal adult if your main stimulation as a child was to be pushed and pulled about constantly and against your will, sometimes painfully and often causing discomfort? To add to this, if anyone remembered to let you play, it was only in a structured and orderly way that never enabled you the opportunity of spontaneous expression. The final insult was that you seemed to spend half your life being carted from one sterile environment to another where men and women in white coats would peer at you without actually noticing that you had any feelings or even that you knew they were there. They would proceed to talk over your head, not about you but about bits of your body and whether you had a mind, and all the while you were unable to express the frustration and confusion you felt at the undignified treatment.

Making choices is an essential part of learning as we grow up. Not all choices made by small children are appropriate, however, and a child with disabilities requires discipline in her life just as a non-disabled child does. It should be appreciated, though, that refusal to acknowledge a child's protests against a plainly uncomfortable experience, which is being administered by the adult to whom she must turn for a role model, may lead that child to lose a very important developmental guide.

As a carer of a child with a disability, you may be asked to carry out appropriate measures in the home to enable your child's development. Some of the advice will be excellent and appropriate to your individual child's needs. Other advice may not be. Parents, therapists, doctors and educators are all professionals who need to work together in real partnership for the benefit of the child. The professionals who offers you advice will probably have a wide experience of similar situations but we are all capable of making mistakes and misinterpreting situations. It is the service of your child's emotional, physical and intellectual needs which is paramount. Professionals who are willing to listen to your views, accept your preferences and amend their advice accordingly are more likely to be able to support you in providing your child with beneficial treatment and training.

A positive attitude towards a child is essential. Children with disabilities (like any children) need praise and encouragement, and to be respected for who they are, not who you might be trying to make them be. You may decide to opt for private therapy or training. For economic reasons you may not have this choice. If you can and do choose this route, remember that you are still the carer and you still control the situation for the benefit of your child.

It used to be very difficult for children who have any but the mildest of disabilities to gain automatic access to ordinary educational opportunities and even more difficult for adults to gain access to properly paid employment. With new legislation in many countries, things are beginning to change with opportunities for attending local mainstream schools and gaining employment protected in law to a greater degree than ever before. However, change will not be complete overnight. There is a need for basic amenities to enable people with disabilities to participate equally. Such amenities include accessible buildings, appropriate equipment and properly trained assistants to help in the classroom or workplace.

Changes internationally in attitude and legislation with regard to inclusion are largely due to dedicated and relentless effort on the part of a number of disability rights organizations which just goes to show what can be achieved by ordinary people where the determination exists.

If you choose to have your child educated in a special school, is it because you are certain that the special environment really offers your child the best hope of an independent future? Or is it because you have been pressured by a local authority whose resources are currently organized with a non-disabled orientation? Do you think their needs will be better met in a segregated environment? My own experience of working with very many children who attend both mainstream and segregated provision is that frustration about resources and needs being met occur in about equal measure in both environments.

The biggest hurdle many people with disabilities face is what happens after the age of 19? Many carers have said to me that this is their biggest worry. At the age of 19 the support which might have been offered within special school melts away and the teenager is suddenly catapulted from a protected, often segregated environment into an adult world which is hostile to his needs. Provision for adults is very varied and highly dependent on the priorities of local social service providers.

Chapter 3

# THE EARLY STAGES

This chapter considers the developmental signs that might indicate a child is not developing according to expected developmental stages and to enable the reader to compare this to the developmental stages we normally expect in early infant development.

## RECOGNIZING THE SYMPTOMS

If your child was born prematurely, had a trauma at birth or had an accident after birth, you will probably have been made aware of the possibility that she could have brain damage. For many people, however, the realization that there is something wrong comes very slowly. The following signs might occur which cause concern for carers.

### Ages one to three months (and older)
The child:

- does not kick
- seems stiff or unduly floppy
- looks asymmetrical – for example, more active on one side than the other
- takes a long time to feed and has poor sucking reflex
- does not smile by ten weeks
- does not meet mother's eyes
- does not follow object held six inches away and moved horizontally.

## Ages three to six months (and older)

The child:

- is still unable to hold up head
- does not put hand in mouth
- has limbs that seem very stiff (as if the muscles were always tight)
- has very floppy limbs
- has head thrown back
- has feet turning out
- crosses legs in scissor action
- has feet pointing at toes rather than flat
- tends to curl up in a foetal position
- tends to throw arms and body backwards
- has eyes rolling backwards or sideways
- does not turn to sound
- is extra sensitive to touch demonstrated by excessive crying on physical contact
- does not seem to recognize familiar people
- is not cooing, gurgling or, later, babbling
- does not reach for objects
- does not roll over from front to side
- dislikes being on stomach and is unable to lift head in this position.

## Difficulty of diagnosing CP in the early months

Many of the signs of cerebral palsy are actually reflexes and responses which are naturally present in a newborn baby but which usually disappear after a few weeks. This makes it very difficult to diagnose CP in the early days of life. It is only as those early reflexes and motor patterns persist past the appropriate age that cause for concern becomes apparent.

## BRIEF OUTLINE OF CHILD DEVELOPMENT

The following outline of average child development is based on the work of Sheridan (1975), Levitt (1977) and others. This outline of developmental progress gives average ages. If your child is not progressing exactly as outlined in this chart there is no automatic need for concern; it is only a guide. However, it is likely that a child who has cerebral palsy (unless very mildly affected) will show significant difference in his development.

### Gross motor (body movements)

| 1–3 months | • Head flops if sat up<br>• Jerky kicks when on back<br>• Becomes less likely to curl up when handled |
|---|---|
| 3–6 months | • Holds head up independently<br>• Leans on forearms and raises head<br>• Can roll from front to side<br>• Can sit up with support |
| 6–9 months | • Can roll from back to stomach<br>• Can sit alone<br>• Pats a mirror image<br>• Goes up on all fours |
| 9–12 months | • Rolls to change positions, lying, sitting, etc.<br>• Crawls<br>• Stands supported<br>• Walks holding on or alone at 12 months |
| 12–18 months | • Walking alone, after walking with one hand held<br>• May begin stiff running<br>• Kneels unaided<br>• Squats at play<br>• Stands and stoops to pick up toy |
| 18–24 months | • Runs less stiffly<br>• Walks up stairs holding on<br>• Throws ball with direction<br>• Walks backwards pulling toy by string |
| 2–2½ years | • Climbs easy apparatus<br>• Kicks large ball<br>• Jumps with two feet together<br>• May be able to tricycle a little |

| 2½ –3 years | • Goes up stairs with alternate feet<br>• Agile climbing<br>• Avoids obstacles<br>• Can run or walk on tiptoe |
|---|---|
| 3–4 years | • Climbs ladders and trees<br>• Stands on one leg for five seconds<br>• Hops on same leg<br>• Throws and catches ball |
| 4–5 years | • Can dance, skip, hop on either leg<br>• Can walk on narrow line |

## Vision and fine motor (hand/eye coordination)

| 1–3 months | • Watches mother's face<br>• Turns to light<br>• Thumb rests in palm<br>• Has automatic grasp but can't let go |
|---|---|
| 3–6 months | • Gazes around and is visually alert<br>• Becomes able to reach out and touch object being looked at<br>• Takes interest in object in hand |
| 6–9 months | • Watches dropped object but forgets it when can no longer see it<br>• Can pass objects from one hand to another<br>• Mouths objects |
| 9–12 months | • Takes object out of container<br>• Quick to visually scan environment and select desired object<br>• Uses fingers in isolation from each other<br>• Prods, pokes and later points with index finger |
| 12–18 months | • Can pick up small crumbs<br>• Can build 2–3 block tower once shown how<br>• Scribbles with crude grasp<br>• Points to pictures and enjoys books<br>• Mouthing objects less |
| 18–24 months | • Removes wrapping from sweets<br>• Circular scribbles and dots<br>• Turns single pages, book right way up |
| 2–2½ years | • Builds tower of 6–8 blocks<br>• Quick recognition of pictures in books<br>• Paints dots, strokes<br>• May hold crayon with first two fingers and thumb |

| 2½–3 years | • Imitates finger play<br>• Can copy a cross and draw body with head and one other part of body<br>• Cuts with scissors<br>• Paints at easel |
|---|---|
| 3–4 years | • Draws a body with head, trunk, legs, arms, fingers<br>• Matches about four colours<br>• Can thread beads |
| 4–5 years | • Copies square, letters<br>• Can draw person and house with detail<br>• Counts fingers<br>• Matches and names colours |

## Hearing and speech

| 1–3 months | • Startles to loud noise<br>• Stills to familiar gentle sounds<br>• Cries when hungry or if uncomfortable |
|---|---|
| 3–6 months | • Coos, gurgles and (by six months) babbles<br>• Turns to sound<br>• Communicates by moving (e.g. begins to raise arms to indicate wish to be picked up) |
| 6–9 months | • Chuckles, laughs, squeals and screams<br>• Turns quickly to mother's voice<br>• Listens attentively<br>• Practises sounds |
| 9–12 months | • Babbles using purposeful sounds<br>• Begins to understand words, gestures. Knows name, 'no' and may say some understandable words. Understands more than says<br>• Waves 'bye-bye' |
| 12–18 months | • Attends to words being spoken. Uses about 6–20 words.<br>• Echoes some words<br>• Obeys simple instructions<br>• Points to body parts<br>• Enjoys nursery jingles<br>• Names of people and things understood |
| 18–24 months | • Uses about 50 words<br>• Refers to self by name and puts two or more words together<br>• Joins in nursery rhymes |

| 2–2½ years | • Uses 200 or more words<br>• Questions and pronouns<br>• Enjoys simple stories<br>• Says some rhymes<br>• Names some body parts<br>• Follows directions, (e.g. up, down, etc.) |
|---|---|
| 2½–3 years | • Listens to story attentively<br>• Others can understand what the child is saying<br>• Often asks for favourite story<br>• Counts with understanding of quantity |
| 3–4 years | • Speech grammar correct<br>• Can describe recent events<br>• Jokes, tells long stories and fantasizes<br>• Counts to 20 |
| 4–5 years | • Fluent speech<br>• Acts out stories<br>• Enjoys jokes |

## Social and emotional self-care

| 1–3 months | • Sleeps frequently<br>• Social smile by eight weeks<br>• Appears alert<br>• Sucks well |
|---|---|
| 3–6 months | • Recognizes people<br>• Can show pleasure and excitement<br>• Lips, tongue and swallowing become active and is capable of dealing with soft food<br>• Hands can be placed on bottle |
| 6–9 months | • Recognizes tone of voice<br>• Responds differently to strangers<br>• Holds bottle or cup and drinks |
| 9–12 months | • Reacts to encouragement<br>• Shows signs of emotions<br>• Plays peek-a-boo and searches for hidden objects<br>• Offers toy to others<br>• Wary of strangers<br>• Holds spoon and may take to mouth but overturns it<br>• Is messy eater; drinks alone if guided and chews<br>• Imitates others |

| 12–18 months | • Picks up cup/spoon and takes to mouth<br>• Puts out arms and legs for dressing<br>• Restless to indicate toilet need<br>• Plays alone but near others<br>• Objects put in and out of containers |
|---|---|
| 18–24 months | • Indicates toilet needs<br>• Able to undress a little<br>• Independent feeding<br>• Make-believe play<br>• Does not realize dangers |
| 2–2½ years | • Eats skilfully with spoon and may use fork<br>• Puts on hat and shoes<br>• Active, restless and rebellious and has tantrums<br>• May join in make-believe play with others<br>• Cannot understand sharing |
| 2½–3 years | • Washes hands but needs help drying<br>• Takes off and puts on clothes except buttons<br>• Likes to help adult<br>• Understands sharing<br>• Left and right confused in dressing |
| 3–4 years | • Can wash and dry hands<br>• Dresses with buttoning but not laces<br>• Takes turns<br>• Appreciates past, present and future<br>• Protective of others |
| 4–5 years | • Knife and fork used<br>• Undresses and dresses<br>• Relates to friends |

## GETTING A DIAGNOSIS

My own research suggests than in 57 per cent of cases, official diagnosis took place six months or more after problems had been picked up by parents. In 29 per cent of cases it took in excess of a year for a diagnosis to be provided. While it is understandable that doctors may be unwilling to diagnose straight away given the incidence of recovery in the early months, I believe that 12 months plus is an unacceptable time-lag and parents are justified in requesting an appraisal of their child's condition if one has not been offered by the age of 12 months. It is usually appropriate for a child to begin being assessed and given exercises by a physiotherapist before a definite diagnosis can be made.

Many parents have reported that they felt the consultant had knowledge of a diagnosis well before they were told. It is extremely helpful if carers can be told as early as possible as it is well documented that early therapeutic intervention can help to limit the damaging effects of cerebral palsy.

Doctors may find the emotional experience of telling a parent that their child has a disability extremely distressing. Added to this their past experience in dealing with severe disability, and feelings of frustration when faced with a disabling condition they know they cannot cure, may result in doctors taking a negative stand in regard to the future of a child with cerebral palsy. Counselling skills are not taught to doctors in any depth and nearly all of their training is geared towards cure through the use of surgery and drugs. This leaves the odds fairly stacked against a positive relationship developing between the carers, who are likely to be highly motivated to do all they can to help their child, and the consultant whose training leaves him in a relatively helpless situation when faced with caring parents and a child whom he is unable to cure.

Reading through comments made by other carers in my own research I was overwhelmed by the almost unanimous opinion that the consultant was/ is unhelpful and unnecessarily negative. In contrast, physiotherapists were seen as supportive and helpful. In many cases the physiotherapist is reported to offer the first positive support carers receive from professionals involved in the care of their child. This enormous body of opinion from clients suggests that the medical professional might benefit from a re-evaluation of the current approach to children with disabilities and their carers.

Fear of overestimating a child's abilities and consequent disappointment to carers, possibly coupled with their own uncertainty regarding a child's future, may lead a doctor to play down a child's potential. I do not want to give the impression that the medical profession is peopled by uncaring and insensitive beings. There is an emphasis on cure and control of disease within medicine. Doctors are trained to focus on impairment and what they can do to reduce the impact or remove impairment altogether. They also have a professional responsibility to ensure that advice given is realistic rather than optimistic. This may lead to caution where prognosis is concerned.

## PARENTS' FIRST REACTIONS AND
## SUPPORT IN THE EARLY DAYS

There are a variety of immediate reactions which a family might have when they realize their child has a permanent disability. How they feel about it will be affected by many influences such as: what personal experience they have of disability, how they are told, what attitudes they already have about disability, whether they had considered the possibility before of having a child who has a disability.

It is commonly believed parents go through a process of grieving which is very similar to the reaction to be expected at the death of a child. This process progresses from shock to anger, guilt and eventually what is termed acceptance. Many books and professionals stress the importance of 'coming to terms with a child's disability'. This may well be a true reflection of the reactions of some parents. However, research carried out by Priscilla Alderson and Chris Goodey between 1987 and 1989 revealed that many parents felt that their feelings were influenced by the attitudes of doctors and other health professionals who talked to them about their children after diagnosis. Unfortunately these attitudes were often negative. 'I'm afraid your child is disabled.' 'I am sorry to have to tell you but . . .' Alderson and Goodey give a number of examples of cases where parents feel that they were prepared for what happened and were willing to welcome their children but where the professionals involved were distressed and uncomfortable, even to the point of crying or being unable to look at the parents when discussing the situation with them. This kind of reaction from professional people who we hope have our best interests at heart can only at best produce confusion and at worst actually create the experience of grief for the parents (Alderson and Goodey 1998).

There is no logical reason for feeling badly towards or about a young child. There may be plenty of reasons to feel unhappy about lack of information, money, advice and practical support, all of which are commonly a problem for families who have a member with a disability. Professional people who encounter the young family getting to grips with having a new member with a disability can make a valuable contribution by adopting a positive attitude and directing the family to sources of support.

Parents of a child with a disability may be thrust into a situation they probably did not expect, which is generally perceived in negative terms and feared with dread by many prospective parents and medical professionals, and about which there may be very little information available. However, many parents report very positive feelings towards, and involvement with, their child. Negative attitudes and beliefs are not likely to change overnight.

The best action parents can take is to make contact with self-help support groups as early as possible so that they can share information and experiences with others in a similar situation. If your health visitor, community nurse or family doctor doesn't know of any in your area, your local cerebral palsy association may be able to help.

I have heard it suggested in some professional circles that parents should be left to get to know their child for a few months before the professionals come into the home offering support and developmental advice. While respect for the privacy of the family is to be applauded, each family is unique in its needs and interpersonal relationships. Given the chance, many families will know what they need most and it may be that the professional involved at the beginning has a role in enabling the family to establish priorities.

The first point of contact is likely to be with the doctor who diagnoses your child. The second point of contact in the UK is likely to be a health visitor. In other countries involvement might come from a community nurse or other community health professional. In a very few areas a special needs health visitor may be available whose responsibility it is to link the hospital input with the community as well as offering carers and children general support in early health care. The family may need help with getting a clearer understanding of their new situation. I refrain from using their terms 'learning to cope with' or 'coming to terms with' because, if handled properly, these negative images of disability can be avoided in the very early stages. I benefited greatly from early contact with adults with cerebral palsy who have busy social lives and successful careers. A number of forward thinking organizations are developing a system whereby role models (adults who have cerebral palsy) meet and offer support and encouragement to younger children with CP (see the Useful Addresses and Contacts section).

# Chapter 4

# MANAGEMENT OF CEREBRAL PALSY

One of the early difficulties will be uncertainty around a child's prognosis (likely outcomes as he grows up). There have been a number of studies designed to establish whether outcomes can be predicted. It has been found that the specific type of cerebral palsy may be an important factor in independent living. However, there are numbers of adults with severe quadriplegia (where medical prognosis is not good) who have fine jobs and good standing in the local community. It has also been found that some children who have sustained minimal damage become severely disabled while others who appear to have sustained severe damage are only slightly affected in motor ability. According to one study, the employment outlook was best for those who had mild spastic paralysis and who had attended regular school. However, it is important to recognize that employment opportunity and other outcomes are as dependent on the construction of the environment as on the development of the individual. I would suggest that these studies are showing which groups are most likely to be able to 'fit into' the non-disabled world rather than any indicator of ability and future prospects given the right community support and opportunity.

In my own study the most popular question parents asked when their children were diagnosed was, 'What will her prospects be?' This was followed in order by, 'Will she walk?', 'What caused it?', 'Can she be cured?', 'How severe is it?', 'Will she be mentally handicapped?', 'Will she talk?', 'What treatment is available?', 'How can I help her?', 'What is cerebral palsy?' and 'Will future children be the same?' These are all difficult questions to answer however experienced the consultant. Quoting statistics on outcomes will not provide a formula for your child's development. So much in any child's life depends on factors unique to that child's situation. The family can help its own children enormously by having a positive attitude towards them and helping them to grow and develop. The medical or child development team can provide backup to families. In the UK, if you do not feel that you are getting enough support, you could try contacting the Scope cerebral palsy helpline (see Useful Addresses and Contacts section) or your local social services department to voice your concerns regarding the support you are receiving.

There can be so much benefit to the family who is listened to, given time, given honest answers to their questions, allowed the opportunity to air their fears and express their emotions and then fully supported, both emotionally and practically, to welcome their child who has disabilities into the family as an equal member with a positive contribution to make.

## GETTING AN EARLY START TO A TREATMENT PROGRAMME

This is a difficult issue. Many parents and carers feel that they have a desperate race against time to do all they can to moderate the effect of their child's brain damage. Others need considerable time to get used to the unexpected situation before contemplating action. Many activists in the disability movement (most of whom have disabilities) believe it is wrong to thrust the young child into programmes of treatment which they see as invasive, cruel and of dubious value.

Some medical studies have suggested that treatment programmes based on exercises have not been proved to be effective but these studies usually accompany research designed to show the effectiveness of the medical interventions such as surgery and drugs. Other studies suggest that the effects of drugs and surgery can be as detrimental as they are likely to be beneficial. The truth of the matter is that no one has yet come up with the magical intervention which can be guaranteed to help children to maximize their potential.

What you can be offered by health professionals will be determined by a number of factors: the resources (money, staff and equipment) available in your area, the attitudes and beliefs of those who provide the service, whether particular methods are preferred by your local service, the type of service delivery, the relationship between your health authority and other sorts of support which might be locally available (such as special interest groups, local branches of Scope, etc.) There are also a number of options available in a private market, which may or may not be beneficial to your child and may or may not be out of reach of your pocket.

## NORMAL LIFE COMES FIRST

Giving your child every opportunity to have a normal life comes before any consideration of special and/or unusual treatments and training programmes designed to support your child's development. Our earliest learning is not achieved by our carers alone inputting information into us. It is now a well-established fact that, from a very early age, children often initiate interaction between themselves and their carers. For example, there have been studies carried out which demonstrated mothers 'teaching' their very small babies to develop early language by copying their child's first babbling. The baby says 'aah ba ga' and the mother responds with 'aahoa ba ba ba ga ga ga'. Without realizing it we are being led by our children into extending their early vocabulary. This process of interaction is augmented by a fairly predictable pattern which most children develop. In their early days this consists mainly of crying followed by feeding followed by sleeping. Gradually the child will spend longer and longer awake and quietly (or loudly in some cases!) attending to the world around him. Later he begins to explore with first his eyes, then his hands. As the child's natural curiosity unfolds, his mobility will increase. Along with this increased mobility comes further opportunity to learn about the small environment in which he lives simply through exploration. By the age of six months, a child is likely to have mastered rolling over to get closer to a desired object and possibly sitting to gain an alternative perspective. By one year, children have developed some means of travelling across small distances to reach a desired object and will be pulling themselves up to get at objects they can't reach from a lying position. By 18 months most children have mastered the art of walking and, once this is achieved, their vocabulary often makes dramatic progress.

All of this takes place without the need for conscious effort on the part of the carer to enable the process. Even if we are preoccupied with other things the child will find a way to discover the world and learn by experience and experiment. A child who has cerebral palsy is disadvantaged from the earliest point of this natural development process, starting with the early emotional life.

Children with cerebral palsy may have difficulty in giving their parents the cues that normally facilitate development in a reciprocal way. If a child is unable to put out the communication which sparks off the necessary adult response, her development could be impeded. We can help reinstate this process with a little thought and appropriate advice. The local educational psychologist, peripatetic teacher, occupational therapist or speech and language therapist may be able to offer some advice on play and ways of being with our children. If you have older children, reminding yourself of the way you interacted with them may help. I found it well worthwhile to invest in a couple of books on child development and play (which were not aimed at children with disabilities) to remind myself on the kind of play activity which might be appropriate for my son Dan's age group.

Lots of stimulation from very early on will aid your child's natural development. This doesn't necessarily mean that you have to be attending to your child every second of the day but it does mean that you will need to provide opportunities. For example, if you are leaving your child to play on her own while you do housework or attend to the needs of another child, surround your child with stimulating toys which move, produce sounds and/or have bright reflective colours. The sounds and bright colours are particularly important if your child is suspected to have difficulties with hearing and vision.

Playing music to small children is also very stimulating. Classical music can be particularly entertaining because it has a complexity which will keep a child's attention. Nursery rhymes are excellent for helping a child to gain a sense of rhythm and producing action through rhythm.

Start reading stories to your child as early as possible. Show her pictures, shapes and puzzles and, most importantly, talk to her. A running commentary on what you are doing will help your child to develop understanding, keep her amused and get her involved in family life.

## TREATMENT AND THERAPIES

Health care for children who have disabilities is theoretically commonly organized by a multidisciplinary team (MDT) based on friendly cooperation between various professionals. Team meetings are held at regular intervals where the progress of individual children will be assessed. This is the most commonly adopted system in the UK. Various criticisms have been made of this system of organization. There tends to be a fragmented approach where each professional dwells on his or her particular expertise rather than a joint effort to support the child's global development. The team leader (often a consultant) may tend to lead discussions and have an overriding control over methods of treatment and, as team meetings are based on reporting work which has been done with the child, there is a tendency to be backward looking rather than having a positive, goal directed approach.

The interdisciplinary team (IDT) is forward looking, works closely together and is goal directed. Members of the team meet to agree goals a child should be able to reach and ways in which they can cooperate towards attaining those goals with the child. Some authorities in the UK are attempting to carry out treatment under this method.

The transdisciplinary team (TDT) is also goal directed and is based on the integration of expertise so that any one member of the team is able to do the job of another member of the team. Under this system one professional can become the main link with the family and build up a close relationship with family and child. This system is virtually unheard of in the UK. The Peto inspired conductive education method practised in Hungary operates on this principle.

The following example demonstrates how these three approaches may differ in relation to self-help in feeding. Under the MDT, feeding might be seen as the domain of the occupational therapist (for appropriate equipment) and the speech and language therapist (for developing appropriate eating patterns). These professionals might give the child self-help practice in specific therapy sessions but, morning and evening, she may be fed (possibly with and possibly without encouragement of self-help) by parents (or house parents in institutions). The IDT might see bringing the spoon to the mouth as a goal. A programme will be discussed to help the child reach this goal and different members of the team will contribute towards this goal during therapy. The occupational therapist might suggest feeding aids which will make the task easier, the speech and language therapist may be able to suggest types of food and communication at meal times which will enhance success, the physiotherapist might suggest ways of encouraging good motor patterns to enable the child to control movement in the task. Under the TDT, training is similar for all members of the team; each is taught to consider all aspects of a child's function and environmental needs. Once the goal is established it easily becomes incorporated into the therapeutic routine of the day. It may be worth finding out from your counsellor or health visitor what kind of teamwork approach is carried out in your area.

## Assessments

During your child's life there will be an ongoing round of assessments made by one or more professionals each with a specific purpose in mind. Some assessments are carried out by members of the team responsible for your child's health care and treatment and some may be carried out at specialist centres. The consultant may lead the local team in routine assessments on a regular basis with the aim of monitoring progress and making adjustments to the child's treatment pattern. In any case individual therapists who see your child regularly are likely to be carrying out regular assessments of their progress even if only informally.

You may be referred to a specialist centre. You might, for example, get a referral to a communication aid centre to assess your child's needs in regard to the most suitable equipment to help her to maximize the effectiveness of her communication or a seating clinic where your child can try out various aids to improve her posture when seated. At one of these centres there is likely to be a brief assessment undertaken by a MDT of professionals working within the centre. They may then produce a report on their observations of your child's abilities and give recommendations regarding the particular need they have been asked to address.

There may be a compulsory assessment procedure which takes place if the decision is made by the local education authority that your child needs a statement of special educational needs (in the UK) or individualized education programme (in the USA) before entering school or while she is at school. This is usually led by an educational psychologist but reports will be requested from all professionals who have regular contact with your child.

Throughout their school life, children will have their educational needs regularly reviewed. In the UK, when a child with a statement is nearing school-leaving age an assessment will be made, at a 14+ review, of their abilities and needs with regard to further education (FE) and possibilities regarding employment.

Individual professionals will make assessments of your child's abilities and needs in regard to their particular area of expertise as and when they feel it is appropriate to do so, or if they are asked to do so by another professional. If you have a need for specially adapted housing or some adaptations in the home an assessment will be made by an occupational therapist to establish what adaptations are needed and they will report to the local housing authority. If your child needs a special mattress to ease pressure, she will need an assessment first, possibly from the community nurse, who can also offer continence advice. Adults seeking employment can be offered assessments from various organizations dealing in work opportunities for people with disabilities.

Assessments of any sort invariably lead to reports being written and distributed to other relevant professionals. In some cases copies of reports will also be sent to the family but this is by no means certain. It is possible, in fact highly likely, that a vast amount of information about your child will be collected and distributed which you will never see, let alone get an opportunity to contribute to, and which will have a direct effect on the kind of options offered to her. You are often entirely reliant on the goodwill of individual professionals as to whether you are invited to see or contribute to reports written about your child. In the UK, USA, Canada, Australia and many other countries, the law does provide some protection in regard to assessments, as partnerships with parents and the right to see reports are now written into the law. However, you may not automatically be offered these options.

The effects that reports, passed on from professional to professional, can have may be extremely helpful in ensuring continuity of care and treatment. However, they may sometimes be detrimental. The key to good report writing is that your child's strengths should be stressed and built upon first and foremost. The family's account of a child's abilities and needs should be given serious consideration since children will often perform tasks more successfully at home, on their own with the family, than when they are under observation from professionals in a contrived situation in which the professional will be placed under a time constraint. Where difficulties are identified they need to be reported in a way which is not offensive and concentrates on positive action which can be taken to overcome obstacles, wherever possible using the child's strengths to enable this. All aspects of the child's life should be taken into account when a report is compiled rather than a concentration on isolated factors. For example, a report from a physiotherapist on good positioning which fails to take account of the seating which is available to the child may fall short. A dietician who advises sugary food to increase weight should be mindful of dentistry advice regarding the care of teeth.

## Action you can take to influence assessments

In the week leading up to the assessment, make a note of everything your child achieves, or problems you observe which you think may have some relevance to the assessment, and report this to the professionals. If you feel able, write your own assessment of your child's abilities and needs and present copies to the professionals who see your child. Ask to be sent a copy of any report which is written. If you receive a copy of a report and there are aspects of it which you do not feel happy with, write to the professionals concerned voicing your concerns. In a serious case, where the report could have long-term negative consequences, in the UK your health service should have a complaints procedure that you should be able to access via your local health provider.

You could involve support from within the Disability Rights Movement. There are a number of organizations which concentrate on the need to protect people with disabilities from unfair treatment and, in some instances, advocates can be made available who will represent you and your child in an official capacity (see the Useful Addresses and Contacts section).

You can ask for a second opinion. However, consultants called in to offer second opinions often know and respect the first consultant and may be unwilling to contradict him. Also, assumptions about a child's abilities are often made on the basis of statistics associated with types of CP rather than an open-minded assessment of that particular child. This could lead to a consensus of opinion among consultants which does not necessarily relate to your own, individual child's development. You can pay for an independent assessment but independent assessments are not likely to carry as much weight with your local providers as their own in-house assessors.

If you can get access to a video camera, regular recording of your child when she is demonstrating her abilities, and any problems she might have, can help professionals to get a more complete picture of your child. Some support groups have video cameras which they hire out very cheaply or free.

There is a great deal of controversy about the best treatment methods for children who have cerebral palsy and individual therapists are bound to have their own opinions and preferences from the wide range of options. You may feel pressured to ignore systems which do not find favour with your therapist. You may even be made to feel that to take a different line would be irresponsible. There are a number of independent but well-respected assessment centres that you could contact for further assistance (see the Useful Addresses and Contacts section).

## PROFESSIONAL ROLES WITHIN THE HEALTH SERVICE

This section applies specifically to the UK but similar systems exist in many countries. For example, in Australia support in the early days of a baby's life is provided by the maternal and child health nurse. In the USA there are well-baby clinics attached to many health centres and paediatricians tend to carry out the regular health checks. In New Zealand the organization PLUNKET offers a range of services for under five-year-olds.

### Health visitor

The health visitor is a state registered nurse (with extra training as a health visitor and possibly in midwifery) who specializes in mother and child health in the community, especially in the very early days of a child's life. Her responsibilities include:

- establishing a relationship with the pregnant woman during the antenatal period

- visiting the mother and baby in the home to note the family circumstances and give advice on aspects of baby care such as feeding and immunization

- identifying families who have special needs
- running sessions at the child health clinic or general practitioner (GP) surgery
- providing health education
- visiting playgroups and nurseries
- liaising with hospital units and links with voluntary bodies
- being a member of, and contributing to, the local MDT dealing with children who have disabilities.

The health visitor is often the most vital link between the family in the home and all other services. She is likely to be the first point of contact you will make in the home. It will often be the health visitor with whom you will discuss your concerns in the first instance. Her training should enable her to help identify where a child's development is not following normal patterns.

Being involved with the family from very early on, the health visitor is best placed to provide early advice and act as a liaison point between the hospital, the GP, other health service professionals and the education service. She can often help out by making referrals for assessment, etc. if you are worried and in need of other professional advice.

## Special needs health visitor

In some health authorities one or more health visitors will take on a special role in supporting families in which there are children with disabilities. This facility is not very widespread but, where they exist, special needs health visitors play a vital role in acting as a contact point between the family, the hospital and the community services. They should be equipped with knowledge, not only about your child's disability, but also about the various statutory and charitable sources of support which are available. Ideally, they will also be able to form a link between hospitals where your child's problem may be initially identified and the community health care which you will come to rely upon to some extent. They should also be able to offer counselling (or advice on where you can go to get counselling) and put you in touch with other families so that you can get support from people in a similar situation early on.

## District nurse

Most community medical practices have a district nurse attached. Otherwise your local hospital or GP can advise you on who to contact. The district nurse can offer help with incontinence (such as the provision of nappies or other continence aids) and can also help provide supportive mattresses for children who might be in danger of getting pressure sores from lying in one position for any length of time. Basically, the district nurse can be called upon to offer support in any of the nursing care functions which are relevant to your child. If the district nurse can't help directly she should be able to refer you to the appropriate professional.

## Paediatric consultant and registrar

The paediatric consultant is a senior doctor who has chosen to specialize in the medical care of children. A paediatric registrar has also chosen to specialize in the medical care of children and is a qualified doctor but at a more junior level than a consultant. The paediatric consultant or registrar will probably be the first specialist you meet when you are aware that your child is not developing to your expectations. Consultants and registrars are based either in hospitals or in community health care practices.

The role of consultants and registrars is to assess your child's physical condition, to provide a diagnosis where possible, to offer appropriate medical treatment to alleviate any difficulties your child is having and to refer your child to other specialists where there is a problem outside the scope of their own specialism.

The early stages will probably be taken up with the consultant or registrar trying to establish how your child is developing physically against what is considered to be normal development.

## Special care unit

The majority of children who have CP will not have experienced obvious problems at birth and their condition is picked up only as they are developing. If a child has serious problems at birth (such as lack of oxygen) the consultant may be concerned, initially, with guarding against such dangers as further brain damage from fits, failing heart, lungs, kidneys and other organs. If it is thought necessary, the child may be monitored in a special care unit where specially trained staff can monitor her heart rate, breathing and other bodily functions. A baby who is born very pre-term may need to be cared for in the baby unit for many weeks.

If a child is experiencing severe convulsions (fits) at birth, precautionary measures may be taken immediately to reduce the risk of further brain damage. Stopping violent fits is a priority and certain drugs (such as phenobarbitone and/or phenytoin) can be administered. These are likely to control fits and may occasionally produce severe side-effects such as extreme drowsiness. The effects of such drugs can make it very difficult for consultants to establish the extent of damage at this point. Another common precaution is to put children in special care on ventilator machines to help with their breathing. This involves assisting the child's breathing by placing a tube through the mouth or nose into the trachea (windpipe). The child might be assisted with early feeding by milk being given through a nasogastric tube which passes through the nose and directly into the stomach.

In the 1980s, before these early interventions were possible, many babies died who would survive today and many more suffered brain damage who would manage to avoid it today. Care needs to be taken when administering intervention. It has been shown that ventilators can cause chest infections, tube feeding can inhibit normal feeding patterns and barbiturates can cause children to become lethargic, depressed and unaware of their environment. As a parent you do not have the medical training to discern whether the treatment being administered is actually necessary or not. You have to rely on the judgement of the consultant. What you can do, however, is to ask questions. Get the staff on the unit to explain why they are taking certain measures, whether there might be negative side-effects and why they feel the importance of the intervention outweighs the side-effect. Try not to be aggressive in your questioning. The staff are genuinely concerned with the welfare of your baby and a relationship of trust between staff and parents is essential.

There will come a point where attempts are made to reduce the child's dependence on these supports and to try and introduce normal patterns. This can be a slow process requiring much patience and persistence, especially if you are trying to introduce sucking at the breast or bottle. The staff at the hospital should be trained to help mothers to establish normal feeding. Even after feeding is established the baby might take a lot longer to drink the required amount of milk than a child who is not disabled. Great care needs to be taken that the child receives enough nutrition right from the start. Help may be available from a breast feeding counsellor (in the UK through the National Childbirth Trust) and from your health visitor as well as the staff in the unit.

## CHILDREN ATTENDING OUTPATIENTS

In the majority of cases the condition will not have been picked up at birth and the child may not begin to make regular visits to the consultant until she is some months old and it has been established that she is having some problems. Children who have been supported in the special care environment are likely to be discharged home with their parents or into another caring environment. Carers and parents may be asked to continue to administer drugs or portable ventilation at home and the child will probably visit outpatients on a regular basis so that the consultant can monitor her progress.

For children who are attending outpatients, one of the consultant's concerns will be to establish whether infant reflexes are staying present beyond the age when they should have disappeared, whether they appear to see and hear and how their muscle tone is developing in addition to organ function (heart, lungs, kidneys, etc.). It is very unlikely that consultants will tell you that they are looking out for signs of cerebral palsy. In cases where there has been an obvious incident this might be because they want to be sure of their facts before they confirm or allay your suspicions. If the referral has come from a parent they will be waiting for the evidence of their own eyes and possibly even offering reassurances that there are no obvious signs of a problem while they deliberate about your child's developmental pattern.

The doctor will be interested to note whether deformities seem to be developing and how the muscle is developing. Possible signs to watch out for include the following:

- subdislocation or dislocation of the hips, varus (slanting towards the mid-line) and spine

- inequality in length of legs

- fixing of joints detected when they are put quickly through a range of motion

- head and trunk flexion (curled up in a foetal position), extension (head and trunk thrown backwards) or rotation (head or trunk twisted to one side or the other)

- shoulders flexed (bunched up), extended (thrown back), abducted (turned outwards), or rotated (turned upwards)

- very tight muscles (increased muscle tone or hypertonia)

- very loose muscles (reduced muscle tone or hypotonia)

- uncoordinated or jerky movements

- lack of visual or auditory attention

- frequent spasms (presenting as sudden, jerky movements).

## GETTING THE DIAGNOSIS

During my own research I found that 63 per cent of respondents had to ask before they were given a diagnosis and that those 63 per cent felt that information was withheld from them. Sixty-one per cent were dissatisfied with the answers to their questions after diagnosis was given. In almost all cases the questions were answered by a consultant.

It is very important not to fall into the trap of blaming the consultants for this apparent breakdown of communication between them and carers. Cerebral palsy is very difficult to diagnose and it is even more difficult to predict the outcome of any specific case.

'She may have brain damage or developmental delay' is often the first indication a consultant will give. As mentioned in the introduction, however, it is impossible for the consultant to predict accurately your child's future from early symptoms. There are even cases where babies seem to be extremely affected physically but appear to make complete recoveries. As time goes on, and if symptoms persist, a consultant may venture to suggest a diagnosis. In addition to cerebral palsy your child might have other complications.

As your child gets older the consultant will be looking to see if any contractures (restriction of joint movement) or deformities (such as curvature of the spine) are developing. It is possible that your child will have been referred to physiotherapy and occupational therapy for appropriate advice on ways of handling and on equipment which can reduce the likelihood of these conditions occurring. This is discussed further on in this chapter. The consultant may also refer your child to a speech and language therapist who can advise with feeding, speech, communication and language development. Referral to a speech and language therapist tends to be slower than to other therapists. If you feel your child would benefit from a speech and language therapist's input you are entitled to self-refer.

There are particular key areas of the body where consultants will be concerned to ensure that abnormality does not persist. Muscles in the arms and legs go in pairs. It is often the case (especially in spastic CP) that one of the pairs will become stretched while the other becomes weakened by this. Neck muscles and back and chest muscles can stretch or become very loose, which may lead to the bones which the muscles support going out of shape. There is particular concern to avoid deformity of the spine, which would create a great impediment to walking. In extreme cases the internal organs can be compromised if contracture is severe. The tendon at the back of the foot (known as the Achilles tendon) can also present severe problems by shortening and pulling the feet out of proportion.

## SURGERY

Some researchers have found that young people with cerebal palsy can achieve walking for the first time in their early teens but this is not always the case. Many factors play a part in whether the child will walk including severity of movement disability in general (Day *et al.* 2004).

Many surgeons would prefer to see contractures avoided and gait and upper limb mobility improved through good physiotherapy. However, there are still numerous instances where surgery is advised. Most surgical procedures involve shortening, lengthening or cutting muscles which are causing bones to distort and severely affecting a patient's ability to function. Instrumentation is also used. This involves the insertion of a rod next to a deformed bone to straighten it. The cause of deformity lies not so much in spastic muscles but in their opponents, which are often weak. The key to successful surgery rests on a sensitive appraisal of the effect any procedure might have in other areas of the body. Many incorrect postures are used to compensate for a fundamental or causative deformity elsewhere. Surgery on the secondary deformity runs the risk of further disabling the patient by removing compensation she may need in order to function. Therefore total gait and posture analysis is advised before any surgical procedure is contemplated.

Some surgeons feel that a child must be motivated to benefit from surgery and must have an intelligence level which will enable them to understand the procedures they will be undergoing.

## Major problems and complications which might arise from surgery

Not all spastic states are produced by cerebral palsy. For example, some metabolic diseases cause spasticity and surgery may not be appropriate in these cases. Accurate diagnosis is therefore essential. Apparently weak muscles may have hidden strengths which could be removed by surgery.

Timing is essential. In the first three or four years of life it may not be possible to establish where the main problems will occur. Ambulation (walking) might be difficult to achieve through surgery after the age of eight years. Multiple surgery (correcting a number of deformities in one operative procedure) avoids repeated hospitalization and anaesthetic but it might be less effective because of the difficulty in evaluating eventual muscle balance.

Goals must be correct: surgery to the extremities (feet and hands) may not be effective if hip and spine deformity are central to the lack of balance. The willing cooperation of patient and parents is fundamental. Whether or not procedures are painful or causing frustration must be taken into account. Patient and parents should be involved in planning for corrective surgery and made totally aware of the purpose and likely outcome of the procedure.

Any surgery is likely to involve lengthy pre- and post-operative care. The application of splints and/or plaster casts are commonly needed. There will also be disruption to education caused by time spent hospitalized and convalescing.

Corrective surgery may be suggested in the following cases. This is not an exhaustive list but represents the more common surgical procedures.

## Spinal deformities

- *Scoliosis:* where the spine has distorted sideways in an S-curve instrumentation (implanting rods) and spinal fusion are sometimes used in this case.

- *Thoracic kyphosis:* where the upper spine has distorted so that the patient has a very rounded back.

- *Lumbar lordosis:* where the lower spine is distorted producing convexity in front – this can cause extreme lower back pain but might also be a compensatory deformity developed as an adaptation to hip flexion.

## Pelvic deformities

- *Increased posterior inclination:* where the pelvis protrudes at the rear.

- *Increased anterior inclination:* where the pelvis protrudes at the front.

- *Pelvic rotation:* where the pelvis is twisted horizontally.

- *Pelvic obliquity:* where the pelvis is distorted at an angle making one thigh appear higher than the other.

## Hip deformities

Hip deformity is the second most common orthopaedic problem in CP (scoliosis being the first). Hip dislocation is the most serious deformity of the hip which can occur. The severity of the hip deformity can be assessed by examining the extent of hip abduction (measured by the distance achievable between legs when held apart); 20 degrees abduction is considered very severe, 35–40 degrees moderate and beyond 40 degrees mild. Normal hip abduction is approximately 80 degrees. It may be possible to avoid dislocation by regular passive abduction through stretching or splinting but this is often supplemented by surgical treatment at some time.

## Knee deformities

Knees are often not straight enough or too straight. This might be secondary to a hip deformity so care should be taken if surgery is being suggested that the primary deformity is being taken into account. Surgical procedures often involve weakening the hamstring muscle.

## Foot and ankle deformities

Equinus is caused by shortening of the Achilles tendon producing a distorted appearance to the foot. Surgical procedures are available to 'lengthen' the contracted muscle.

## Hand and wrist deformities

The infant 'thumb in palm' reflex commonly persists in CP and 'fisting' is common. Also, the wrist may become flexed (bunched up) or extended (stretched back). There are a number of procedures which may help to correct hand and wrist deformities by shortening or lengthening certain muscles.

## Plaster-casting and splinting

These procedures may be used post-operatively or, in some case, instead of surgery. Plaster-casting can be used to reduce tone to help avoid contracture but it fails to improve function because the immobility of the limbs in plaster-cast can further weaken muscles. Splinting is a procedure of holding limbs in place with splints. This procedure may be used post-operatively. Children often find splints uncomfortable and may be expected to sleep in them.

If surgery is suggested it is essential that the consultant is questioned closely on the purpose and alternatives. If you are not fully satisfied, ask for a second opinion.

## The UPsuit as a complement to managing posture

The UPsuit is individually designed and consists of a lycra, body splint with plastic boning for extra support. More information is available at www. secondskin.com.au. The difference between the UPsuit and more traditional interventions is that the device provides support and control while allowing movement – it is dynamic. It is claimed that as the user experiences 'normal' movements these movements can be learnt. The UPsuit is a full body suit but there are also other splinting options available including arm, leg and trunk splints.

## Gait analysis

Guy's Hospital in London has developed a gait analysis system which involves substantial input from physiotherapists and an analysis of a child's total muscle involvement and use. Surgical, pharmaceutical and therapeutic interventions are recommended in reports from this laboratory.

## Selective dorsal rhizotomy

Selective dorsal rhizotomy is a new development in the UK although the operation has been available in the USA for a number of years. There is more detailed information about the use of this technique in the USA at this website: www.stlouischildrens.org/content/medservices/aboutselectivedorsalrhizotomy. It involves cutting spastic afferent rootlets to the central nervous system with the aim of reducing spastic tone generally. In the UK, the procedure is being carried out at the Robert and Agnes Hunt Hospital in Oswestry, Shropshire.

## Botox injections

Injections of Botox (botulinum toxin) in minute amounts effectively 'paralyse' the spastic muscle(s) giving the weaker, non-spastic muscles a chance to strengthen. Botox is usually prescribed and administered to specific muscle groups for a specific functional purpose such as walking. Botox injections are nerve blockers, similar to phenol injections but safer in most applications. Because it is reversible (it wears off in a matter of months), it can be used as a rough predictor of muscle- and tendon-release surgery. It is not considered a long-term fix for orthopaedic problems but shows promise as a means to delay or minimize surgery.

## Gastrostomy

Gastrostomy is a procedure that is becoming popular as an alternative to oral feeding where a number of difficulties associated with feeding are found. Difficulties might include: lack of gag reflex (to help cough up food that has gone down the wrong way), extreme difficulty in chewing and swallowing, reflux (acid indigestion), aspiration (where food and drink regularly enters the lungs) and difficulty with weight gain. Gastrostomy involves the insertion of a tube directly into the stomach so that the nutrients necessary to life can be administered directly to the stomach. As more is understood about the difficulties that children with severe CP might encounter with eating in the normal way, this is becoming a very popular procedure. For some children, it may be the only way that they will be able to survive. For other children, the decision for parents is more difficult. There are dangers attached to the procedure. It is imperative that the site of the gastrostomy tube is kept clean and, even then, infection can occur. Reflux is not always cured by gastrostomy and might even be made worse in some cases. There is an increase in the need for subsequent operations with the attendant dangers of undergoing anaesthesia. Studies that have been done into the effectiveness of this procedure have found that one of the main benefits is to the carers in that the demands of feeding routines are lessened. Other recent research has found that while serious complications can arise with gastrostomy, it is safe in 95 per cent of cases (Sullivan *et al.* 2005).

## SPECIFIC THERAPIES

### The team of therapists

In most areas the team of therapists consists of a physiotherapist, an occupational therapist and a speech and language therapist. How early any of these therapists get involved in your child's treatment needs depends on the number of therapists available in the area, the severity and nature of your child's disability and the cohesion of the referral system in your area. My research suggests that physiotherapists are likely to see all children who are diagnosed or suspected of having cerebral palsy. Other therapists are likely to be brought in as and when and if their input is considered necessary.

The therapists are all interested in your child's development but from different perspectives. Physiotherapists are most concerned with the development of your child's movements (motor ability), ensuring that deformity and contractures do not occur and that preventive measures are taken regarding dislocation of joints. Occupational therapists are primarily concerned with the development of your child's ability to help himself and with advising which appliances and equipment can support this. Speech and language therapists concentrate on your child's language and communication development, although they are increasingly becoming interested in children's feeding patterns because the motor skills required for both eating and communicating have some crossover. All three are likely to use development check lists based on 'average, normal development'. There is no such thing as a standard rate of development. Every child is an individual and no child follows an exact developmental pattern but there are certain milestones (activities such as 'sitting up unaided', 'rolling over from back to tummy') which tend to occur at roughly the same age for most children.

## The physiotherapist

A referral to a physiotherapist is often the earliest referral made. The job of 'the physio' is to help a child's mobility to develop and to carry out and teach exercises designed to avoid contractures and bone deformity and unwanted movement. Physiotherapists are sometimes able to offer exercises which will help to reduce spasm in children who experience it, quite common in medium to severe situations. They may also be able to suggest exercises to improve breathing patterns.

There are very many different techniques which can be applied by physiotherapists. In general, they are trained to work with individuals to enable them to obtain maximum physical function but this can be done in a variety of ways. Physiotherapists receive very little paediatric training. Traditionally, physiotherapy has concentrated on isolated areas of dysfunction and worked on the area where dysfunction occurs in an attempt to eliminate it. This is because physiotherapy often tends to be applied to people who have a temporary rather than a permanent disability. For example, if someone has a broken arm, there are certain exercises which can be carried out to help the person regain function in the arm more quickly than he might have done without exercise. However, cerebral palsy is more complex than this. It is a permanent disorder which is caused by a dysfunction of the brain rather than the limbs and muscles. A physiotherapist working with a child who has cerebral palsy has to recognize that this child will probably need to carry out some form of exercise for most of his life. These days physiotherapists tend to specialize so that they are likely to be aware that they are dealing with a long-term problem which will require constant monitoring.

Certain equipment is the remit of the physiotherapist. There is often a grey area between the role of the physiotherapist and the occupational therapist in regard to certain equipment but a physiotherapist could be expected to get involved in the provision of standing frames, wedges, adapted bikes and trikes and other mobility and posture aids which have a direct effect on a child's physical progress and support. In some areas the physiotherapist is considered to be responsible for adaptations to support from the waist down while the occupational therapist is responsible for adaptations to support from the waist up.

## CONDUCTIVE EDUCATION AND PHYSIOTHERAPY

Ester Cotton was a physiotherapist who was very involved in the conductive education movement and who had considerable influence in introducing this type of training into the UK. This is discussed in detail in Chapter 10 on education; I will not dwell on this technique in this chapter because the approach is very different from mainstream physiotherapy and not considered, by those who practise it, to be a therapy so much as an educational process. Conductive education approaches cerebral palsy as a learning difficulty. The central philosophy of conductive education is that a child who has cerebral palsy has a learning problem which may be overcome with repeated practice of everyday activities carried out in an environment which is, as nearly as possible, like the environment the majority of children grow up in. Wheelchairs and other adaptations are avoided if possible and the child learns all of the activities necessary for living from one person who is trained in all of his needs, such as mobility, communication and pre-school play. This person is called a 'conductor'.

## BOBATH PHYSIOTHERAPY

Bobath physiotherapy is a very popular 'early intervention' method (also known as neurodevelopmental treatment – NDT) because it attempts to inhibit unnatural reflexes and movements from the time they arise. Treatment is thought to be most effective if started as soon as there is any indication of a suspected diagnosis of CP. Professor Karel Bobath (a medical practitioner) and his wife Berta Bobath (a physiotherapist) were developing this method for some 30 years up until their deaths in the 1980s.

The Bobath technique seeks to eliminate the infant reflexes which persist in a child who has CP but which normally disappear after a short period of time. Examples of this are: the tendency small babies have to 'fist' their hands, a tendency to turn the head in the opposite direction when they reach out with the opposite arm (known as atonic neck reflex – ATNR) and the head being constantly thrown back.

The treatment programme consists of passive positioning of the child in postures devised to reduce spasticity and unwanted movement. At the same time it tries to give the child a sensation of normal movement (e.g. by facilitating the automatic righting reaction) and implementing the stages of normal development from rolling, through sitting, kneeling, crawling and standing to walking. In later years, the Bobaths concluded that they had been overrating the importance of the abnormal reflexes in assessments and that the normal development sequence does not have to be followed too closely.

It is central to the Bobath concept that skills in handling the child to enable the best possible posture and mobility are transferred to parents so that they can be aware of this throughout the normal day. Although my own son has not followed a rigid Bobath regime I am glad to this day that we had early advice from physiotherapists who were Bobath trained. Because of the advice we received early on we have never allowed his posture to be compromised and I think that this has been essential to his good health and progress over the years.

Nancie Finnie (a physiotherapist and a strong supporter of this method) has written a book called *Handling the Young Child with Cerebral Palsy at Home* which explains ways of handling a child in the day to day home environment that will help to inhibit 'abnormal' motor patterns (Finnie 1997).

The Bobath Centres in London, Scotland and Wales offer assessment and treatment to British children through referral from a paediatric consultant or GP. There is a waiting list. For details of the Bobath Centre in USA and for other Bobath publications see the Useful Addresses and Contacts section.

MOVE (MOBILITY OPPORTUNITIES VIA EDUCATION)

MOVE is a system which aims to integrate teaching, therapy, care and nursing skills to enable the acquisition of motor skills to take place. A programme is devised for each individual which supports them in naturally practising their motor skills within the context of their usual educational and leisure activities. MOVE is based on teaming the expertise of therapy and education to address the functional needs of students when they become adults. Equipment to support a MOVE programme is available from the Rifton Manufacturing Company, details in the Useful Addresses and Contacts section. The equipment places students in positions for performing functional activities such as moving from one place to another, self-feeding, self-controlled toileting, table work and leisure activities.

The equipment allows the staff to physically manage the student while teaching appropriate movement patterns. The equipment allows the students to practise motor skills independently and is designed to help improve their bone and joint health and to increase the muscle strength of the extensor musculature of the body. The MOVE programme is designed so that it can be carried out by anyone who has a care or pastoral role in the child's life and a two day basic training is offered which enables participants to start using a MOVE programme (see the Useful Addresses and Contacts section).

## Occupational therapist

Occupational therapists are trained to look at self-help and specialist equipment which will be likely to enhance or promote self-help in the child. They become involved in helping their clients to have appropriate adaptations made to the environment in which they live to facilitate independence, as well as assisting clients in adapting to their environment.

Some children who have CP will not need specialist equipment. For those who do, the occupational therapist may get involved in any of the following activities: advising on the best cups, spoons, etc. to enable easy feeding, providing seating (or adapting existing seating) to give your child maximum support, lending or suggesting toys to aid development, providing or suggesting suitable pushchairs (or adapting existing ones), advice on wheelchairs, walking frames, standing frames and side lying boards and adapting equipment a child uses in everyday life to suit his physical developmental needs. Additionally, the occupational therapist is trained to suggest appropriate adaptations to the home and community to facilitate independence.

Your child's buggy or wheelchair needs to offer sufficient support to avoid any damage being done to their posture. Some children are fine in an ordinary buggy or wheelchair. For others a buggy or wheelchair can be made more supportive with creative use of foam. Some children will benefit from specially adapted seating. Unfortunately, many of the commonly available special buggies and wheelchairs don't fold and are very bulky. Some buggies double up as car seats but this is not very helpful for those who have to rely on public transport. Wheelchairs can be offered to young children but they are difficult to get and tend to come in standard issue which may not be appropriate to your child's individual needs. There have been some advances in recent years and more supportive wheelchairs and inserts are being developed such as the Jay seating system (see the Useful Addresses and Contacts section), which can be fitted to a standard wheelchair. There are a great variety of special chairs.

When you are considering your child's seating needs it is important that you get a clear idea of what you're hoping the special seating will achieve. Some seating is very bulky. Many special seats have trays in front of them which mean that the child is unable to join the rest of the family at the dining table. Many chairs available on the market depend on numerous straps to hold the child in place. I don't think I would have been very comfortable as a child if several parts of my body were strapped down every time I sat in a chair. On the other hand, chairs which do not rely on straps probably require the child to put in some effort to keep his posture correct. Thus sitting down becomes an activity requiring work rather than one of relaxation. If your child clearly needs special seating it might be worth considering the option of more than one chair, perhaps one for relaxing and one for active sitting. It is unlikely that your local authority will fund more than one chair however.

There are a number of centres which specialize in seating and your physiotherapist or occupational therapist may be able to get you a referral to one of these centres.

It is often considered important for children to stand for a period of time each day. This is because taking weight through the feet helps the proper development of the hip joint which, in turn, helps to prevent dislocation. If a child is unable to stand without support, there are a variety of standing frames available. Other ways to help children with standing practice include holding them in a standing position, giving them some support with your hands while they lean on a sofa or low table and helping them to hold on to a bar or ladder backed chair while they are in the standing position. Not all children will be able to manage these more independent ways of standing, but for those who can there is the added benefit of achievement through their own efforts.

Toilet seats and supportive potties can help a child to develop important independent function. As a child gets older and bigger, adaptations in the home might be needed. These could include hoists and grab rails for bathing, special beds which you can lower and raise to facilitate dressing, ramps and stair lifts.

My research suggests that only about 54 per cent of parents whose children have cerebral palsy receive advice from an occupational therapist, and only 32 per cent of these see one after their child has reached the age of two years.

An overview of what is available can be achieved by visits to exhibitions where manufacturers bring equipment to demonstrate. In the UK the Naidex exhibition is held annually. You can find details at: www.naidex. co.uk. Alternatively you can see some examples of equipment at a specialist centre such as the Disabled Living Foundation. Similar organizations and exhibitions exist in many other countries (see list of Useful Addresses and Contacts section).

The magazine *Disability Now*, published monthly from the Scope office and available online at www.disabilitynow.org.uk, advertises these events and does a helpful review of each one. At these exhibitions you have the opportunity to see an item, possibly try it out and talk to representatives from supplying firms about your particular needs. You can then ask your own therapist to arrange for an assessment of items you are interested in.

Some firms are willing to come out with equipment even if you are not able to involve a therapist, but you need to be sure that you feel confident about your child's physical support needs.

## Speech and language therapist

Speech and language therapists are primarily concerned with children's communication. Communication is a two-way process so speech therapists will be just as interested in how much children can understand as how much they can communicate to the outside world. They are concerned with establishing how a child understands language, whether he can understand verbal instructions or whether he needs clues from his environment to understand what is going on around him. The speech and language therapist will be concerned to give the child some means of communication to the outside world within his particular capabilities. This might be through activities which encourage speech or signing, or the use of electronic aids or picture boards. Sometimes the use of extra aids to speech (like signing) will support the development of vocal communication. Children with cerebral palsy (even in mild cases) often tend to be slow in developing verbal communication. Research has shown that children who are helped to communicate using appropriate aids are often more successful at developing speech as well (Romski and Sevcik 1993).

Speech and language therapists often get involved in helping the child with feeding as it is believed that good feeding patterns are helpful for the possibility of developing normal speech. This is because the same muscles are involved in both activities. There is also a concern that children who have difficulty with feeding might aspirate (where tiny particles of food or drink enter the lungs making chest infections more likely). A speech and language therapist may be able to advise on the consistency and texture of food and drink to avoid this happening.

## Peripatetic teacher

There are some areas where peripatetic teaching is available for your child from a very early age. A good peripatetic teacher can help you and your child to find ways of providing necessary stimulation within the constraints of her physical disability. Some teaching systems have an integrated approach in that they view disability as a learning problem to be overcome alongside other developmental milestones (see Chapter 10). Even if your child is still very small there are educational opportunities she may be able to take advantage of (such as the portage system) so you are advised to read

Chapter 10 even if your child is still very young. A good peripatetic teacher can be a great complement to the work being carried out by the speech and language therapist.

## Psychologist

Psychology is a social science which attempts to base itself on the objective techniques developed in the physical sciences such as physics, chemistry and biology. Psychologists are employed in the assessment of children who are considered to have special needs with a principal interest in their learning ability, their behaviour and their understanding.

It is likely that your child will be assessed at various times by a psychologist, and the psychologist's reports can have a significant effect on the opportunities offered to your child. An educational psychologist may be called in to do assessments on children when entering school, monitor their development within school and provide guidance regarding their further education as emerging young adults. A clinical psychologist or an educational psychologist might become involved with children who appear to have behavioural difficulties.

There is much controversy and debate within psychology on the most appropriate methods to assess ability and behaviour. A widely used method is based on IQ, personality and sociability, which is carried out on the basis of scoring children against a very rigid set of tests. To succeed in these tests children need to be physically mobile, have all their senses (such as sight and hearing) in perfect working order and to have developed an ability to communicate effectively. The child who has cerebral palsy is immediately put at a disadvantage because she is likely to have limitations in one or more of the areas of function upon which psychology testing is based.

More enlightened psychologists will carry out much of their assessment in a more informal way by observing the child in a natural setting on a number of occasions and over a period of time. They will also talk to the parents to gain insight into the parents' view of their child's abilities (Rea-Dickins and Poehner 2011).

There has been a recent shift within psychology towards dynamic assessment (DA) rather than static assessment. DA may offer more flexible tools for assessment of ability in students who have communication difficulties. In DA we measure what a person achieves with appropriate intervention. If the person we are assessing does not appear to be able to do something the skill is taught using approaches that best suit the person who is then retested to see if the intervention was successful. The intervention offered is known as mediated learning.

Lantolf and Poehner (2011) found that DA applied to learners of English as a second language was successful when the teacher applied it in the context of her knowledge of her students and the constraints of her classroom. This supports a flexible application of DA which takes account of individual circumstances.

According to Fuchs *et al.* 2011):

> DA has been described as the assessment of learning potential, mediated learning, testing the limits, mediated assessment, and assisted learning and transfer by graduated prompts. Across these various conceptions, DA differs from traditional testing in terms of the nature of the examiner–student relationship, content of feedback, and emphasis on process rather than product. In traditional testing, the examiner is a neutral participant who provides standardized directions but not, typically, performance-contingent feedback. Many DA examiners, by contrast, not only give performance-contingent feedback but also offer instruction in response to student failure to alter or enhance the student's performance. Put differently, traditional testing is oriented toward the product (i.e., level of performance) of student learning, whereas the DA examiner's interest is in both the product and the process (i.e., rate of growth) of the learning. Some claim this twin focus on the level and rate of learning makes DA a better predictor of future performance. It may help decrease the number of 'false positives,' or children who seem at risk but who, with timely instruction, may respond relatively quickly and perform within acceptable limits. As mentioned, data from DA may also help identify the type and intensity of intervention necessary for academic success. It incorporates a test–teach–test format, conceptually similar to RTI techniques. However, it can potentially measure one's responsiveness within a much shorter time frame. (Fuchs *et al.* 2011, p.340)

An educational psychologist is likely to take the lead in assessing your child's educational needs as school age approaches. It is worth finding out how much the individual psychologist knows about cerebral palsy. If you feel they are not experienced enough, you should feel able to challenge their involvement and ask for someone with some expertise in the field. Even if they do have experience, you should feel confident that your involvement and your knowledge about your child will be taken on board.

## Social worker

Not all families will have regular, or even any, contact with a social worker. In the UK social workers are employed by local social service departments and it is their job to help families and individuals by providing them with access to practical support in the community. Social workers in the USA operate in a similar way to those in the UK as described by their national body: www.socialworkers.org. Social workers are also employed to be aware of and keep an eye on anyone who is considered to be vulnerable in their locality and to intervene if their client seems to be in imminent danger.

If a child has disabilities his family may be offered support from a social worker but usually only if there is some other reason to suppose that the family is vulnerable beyond the simple fact of disability. Examples might be single parent families, families where the social services have reason to believe that the child might be being abused or in danger of abuse, families who have had previous contact with social services, or perhaps by self-referral or referral from another professional.

Another role social workers have is to place children in foster care and to organize adoption. In the UK children who are fostered, adopted or brought up in residential homes will be under the care of a social worker who will be trying to ensure that the child's needs are being met adequately by the arrangements which are being made for them.

In the UK your social worker should be able to find out what benefits you are entitled to and how you can go about claiming them. Your health visitor may also be able to advise you in this area if you do not have a social worker.

## Counsellor

The consultant who sees your child, or your GP, can refer you for counselling or you can self-refer. Basically, counselling involves regular visits to a trained counsellor whose role is to help you to understand, cope with and eventually overcome any negative feelings you may have about your family's circumstances. It is also an opportunity for carers to have their needs acknowledged. It's often the case that the needs of your child seem so overwhelming that your own can get submerged. The end result of this is often that the stress of submerging your own needs can lead to depression or other health problems. You might also be able to seek support from a psychotherapist. Psychotherapists are also trained to help you to overcome any negative feelings you may be experiencing but they are likely to do this in a less directive way than a counsellor. If you self-refer to a counsellor or psychotherapist you may have to go privately and have to pay.

# COMMUNITY INVOLVEMENT

## Under-fives provision

It is well worth finding out if there are any mother and toddler groups in your area. If you want your child to have an equal place in the community, integration needs to begin very early. Giving your child the opportunity to meet and play with non-disabled toddlers who live in the locality is a good starting place. It's also an opportunity for you to get out and meet other mums with small children. So often carers of small children with disabilities become isolated and this isolation can be passed on to the child.

It is also worth finding out whether there are any under-fives groups locally who specialize in catering for children with disabilities. Such playgroups often have specially adapted toys and playgroup sessions which aim to help your child with her early development. If you do manage to find a specialist playgroup it is still worth trying to get into a mainstream toddler group as well. It will help your child's later integration if she is mixing with both disabled and non-disabled children alike from the start.

## Music and art therapy

Music and art are artistic media that are enjoyable to children and both can be used to support a child's development in a number of ways. Through music, a child can express her emotions, develop a sense of rhythm (which will in turn support her physical development), develop her communication skills, benefit from auditory and tactile (through vibration) stimulation and relax. Through art, a child can express emotion, improve fine motor control, practise valuable pre-school skills and benefit from the tactile and visual stimulation of different artistic media. These are just some of the benefits.

You don't have to wait until you have made contact with a specialist to give your child experience in art and music. To play music all you need are instruments (homemade ones will do) and a cassette player. Shakers made of plastic washing up bottles filled with rice grains, upside-down saucepans and wooden spoons, and milk bottle tops on string can provide you with a percussion section. Alternatively you can buy percussion instruments such as maracas, tambourines and drums. Give your child a range of music to enjoy from classical to pop, nursery rhymes to reggae. To enjoy art all you need is paper, paints, non-toxic glue and a variety of materials (cloth, milk bottle tops, pasta, rice, lentils). Play dough, plasticine and clay can all be used for model building.

You can seek specialist advice in these areas. To find out more about music therapy in the UK you can contact the British Society for Music Therapy or the Nordoff-Robbins Music Therapy Centre. To find out more about art therapy in the UK you can contact the British Association of Art Therapy. In the USA the American Music Therapy Association may be able to offer support. In Australia there is the Australian Music Therapy Association and an Australian branch of Nordoff-Robins (see the Useful Addresses and Contacts section).

## Soundbeam

This is a recent development using new technology. Soundbeam uses ultrasonic sensors to pick up movements and translate them into sound. The equipment is so sensitive that the smallest movement (such as an eye blink) can control the sound. I have observed a number of young people with movement difficulties using this equipment and the increase in their range of movement and control over movement has been very evident. My own son has already learnt to control the sound to produce repeating musical patterns with his eyebrows. Another young man, with less severe hemiplegia, has used Soundbeam to increase control in his affected hand. This is an exciting development in leisure and creative opportunities for people with CP who have limitations of movement. It is possible to use Soundbeam to produce sophisticated musical pieces as well as in making fun sounds. For suppliers see the Useful Addresses and Contacts section.

## Respite care

A potentially vulnerable situation can be avoided by offer of regular respite care. There are generally two types of respite care available. Either a trained foster mother can look after your child for occasional or more regular periods of time or the same facility can be offered by some residential homes. The main aim is to give the family a break so that they can care more effectively for their child at home. However, the majority of families are not offered this facility until their child is older. It is likely that a great deal of stress will have built up by the time respite care becomes an option. Many families would not find it easy to part with their child even for a short while and even when they plainly need a break. This is understandable as the closest members of the child's family will often understand their needs much better than strangers. For this reason it is important to try to arrange respite care where your child will get to know someone and the carer will likewise get to know your child so that you can rest assured she is being looked after to your satisfaction. It is a good idea to make sure the temporary carer has all of your child's particular needs and ways of communicating explained to her. It will help to arrange to go on short visits with your child, at first only leaving her for a short while each time until she has built up a relationship with the carer who will provide respite. If you are not happy with the arrangements being offered, it is important that you say so right away so that an alternative can be sought. It can take many months to establish respite care so it's wise to investigate this option before you get exhausted to breaking point. This service is usually offered through a social worker.

## SYSTEMS LESS WIDELY AVAILABLE THROUGH THE NATIONAL HEALTH SERVICE IN THE UK

### Doman-Delacato: patterning

Glenn Doman was a physiotherapist who worked in the late 1940s with Carl Delacato (an educator) and Robert Doman (a physician specializing in physical rehabilitation). A growing body of evidence, which found that sensory enrichment as well as sensory deprivation can alter the structure of the brain, inspired Glenn Doman to develop a technique which aims to treat the brain by altering the neurological (the function of the web of tissues and branching cells which support the nerve fibres and cells of the nervous system) within the brain.

Prior to the introduction of the Doman-Delacato system of treatment, there had been an assumption that brain damage was irreversible and treatment centred on inhibiting symptoms of brain damage (such as abnormal movement). The Doman-Delacato principle is that it is possible to treat the brain itself to enable function to be restored naturally through the restoration of the brain's capacity to dictate appropriate function. To put it more simply, this treatment rests on the theory that when a part of the brain is damaged, other parts of the brain are capable of taking over the function of the damaged area. However, this may not occur naturally and the 'patterning' therapy is designed to stimulate the functioning parts of the brain to develop and to take over the job of those parts of the brain which have been damaged (www.delacato.net/).

There is a vast amount of research which suggests that the actual structure of the brain is changed and its development enhanced by external factors. For example, crawling has been shown to stimulate the firing of secondary motor neurons in the brain. It has been postulated that crawling helps the brain develop properly. Similarly, the tendency children have of enjoying 'spinning round until they are dizzy' and falling over laughing has a very functional purpose. It helps children to develop balance in later life.

The basic principle behind patterning is that mobility is attained only through movement. In addition, where a child has disabilities which interrupt the normal development process, that movement needs to be frequent, intense and repetitive. The Doman-Delacato method also emphasizes the importance of sensory and intellectual stimulation as part of a rounded programme of activities tailored to suit the needs of each individual child and maximize their developmental potential (Doman 1991).

The first institute to provide patterning was the Institute of Human Potential in Philadelphia, USA, where Doman set up the practice. The programme involves short, sharp bursts of activity to be carried out at very regular intervals, in exactly the same way, for a number of times each day. Activities usually last for between one and five minutes each and are carried out in rapid succession. Examples of the kinds of exercises include:

- *Masking:* wearing a mask, for about a minute, which has a valve at the bottom to control oxygen intake and encourage your child to breath more deeply.

- *Cross pattern:* this involves three people: one on each side of the child and the third person turning the child's head. The child is then moved through the action of crawling for a specified number of minutes.

- *Walking with ladders:* this involves aiding the child to walk under horizontal ladders, holding on to the ladder above his head to help steady himself as he takes each step.

- *Arm unlocking and hip unlocking:* these are exercises for stretching and loosening the arms, legs and hip joints.

- *Stand ups:* the child practises standing from a seated position on the adult's lap; the adult is kneeling.

The above are just a few example exercises. An individual programme is developed for each child depending on their particular needs. The programme often involves a number of volunteers who are willing to commit themselves to learning the exercises and coming into the home to carry them out on a regular basis. The institute offers advice on ways to recruit volunteers but a fair amount of resourcefulness, organization and determination is required of the family. Having support and input from volunteers can be an uplifting experience but, on the other hand, it can become very wearing to be constantly interacting with visitors whatever your mood that day. Patterning can be particularly stressful for 'private' people.

## Votja method

The Votja method is based on the work of Temple Fay and is aligned to other similar approaches outlined in this chapter such as sensory integration. Although the originators of some of these approaches date back a long way their influence is still felt today..

The theory behind it is that the child with cerebral palsy has the same reflex movements that can be provoked in the non-disabled newborn child. The treatment programme elicits patterns of reflex motion by manual pressure on 'trigger zones' to induce reflex patterns such as creeping and turning. These patterns of motion are then expected to be 'imprinted' in the central nervous system, stored within the brain and thereby allow normal motor patterns to occur. Parents are instructed in the method so that assessment is necessary only every few weeks. Dr Vaclav Vojta was a Czechoslovakian neurologist who developed his theory in the 1960s and carried out his research in Germany. His theory is based on the evaluation of child development and the idea that the nervous system is able to receive stimulation which affects maturation. The aim is to modify reflex activity so that motor and sensory activity is developed. More information is available at: www.physiobob. com/forum/paediatric-physiotherapy/457-vojta-therapy-cp. Votja advised that treatment should cease if no improvement is seen within a year of commencing treatment.

## Ayres sensory integrative therapy

Dr Anna Jean Ayres was an occupational therapist and educational psychologist who formulated a theory that sensory integrative dysfunction played a significant role in the problems experienced by children who had a neural disorder. She developed diagnostic tools and proposed a therapeutic approach which led to the development of the not-for-profit organization Sensory Integration International in 1972.

Ayres sensory integrative therapy aims to stimulate sensory experience via a set of exercises. In sensory integration theory the senses that are normally below the level of awareness are of prime importance. These include the vestibular sense, proprioception, tactile sensation and kinaesthetic sensation. The vestibular system detects motion, gravity and provides us with our sense of balance. When the influences of vestibular stimuli fail to reach their natural destinations, they cannot adequately contribute to sensory integration. Hypersensitivity to movement and fear of movement are both indicators of a vestibular disorder. Children who excessively crave movement and appear never to get dizzy also may have disorders of the vestibular system. Muscle tone can also be influenced by the vestibular system and when the vestibular system in not integrating information adequately it can contribute to hypotonia. The vestibular system also supports the development of bilateral coordination, which is the ability of the body to use both sides in a coordinated manner, the development of laterality, and the specialization of each side of the body. The vestibular system is anatomically joined with the cochlea system, and it has many close neuronal associations with the pathways for auditory processing and language. Decreased vestibular processing can affect speech and language development. Tactile perception refers to touch. The two sensory systems for touch perception are the protective system and the discriminative system. The protective system responds to light or unexpected touch and alerts us to any stimuli that might be harmful. The discriminative system enables us to gain information about our environment through our skin. It helps us feel the difference between hard and soft, smooth and rough.

Our proprioceptors give us information about the position of our body parts. These receptors are located in our muscles, tendons, ligaments and joints. We don't have to look at our arms and legs to know where they are and exactly what position they are in.

Gravitational security is our feeling of security when we are moving our body in space and in changing our relationship to gravity.

Motor planning or praxis is the ability of the brain to conceive, organize, and carry out a sequence of unfamiliar actions.

According to this method children with CP are unable to integrate the sensory inputs (tactile and proprioceptive) from their trunk and limbs. Consequently the vestibular system fails to provide correct information about the movement of the limbs and posture. Thus, primitive reflexes persist and the child is unable to plan their motor activity. The treatment is one of passive and tactile and proprioceptive stimulation, which should enable the brain to reprogramme and make new connections.

## Vibro-acoustic therapy

Vibro-acoustics can be used as a treatment system for stiff muscles and impaired circulation. It is a further development of music therapy which combines vibrations produced by low frequency sine tones with therapeutic music. The patient relaxes in a chair, or on a bed, which has speakers built into it. Half of the speakers emit low frequency sound waves and the other half play relaxing music. Research trials have been carried out in the use of vibro-acoustics at Harperbury Hospital (now closed) under the direction of music therapist Tony Wigram and physiotherapist Lynn Weaks. Dr Wigram's doctoral thesis can be found at: www.wfmt.info/Musictherapyworld/

modules/archive/stuff/papers/Wigram.pdf. Regular use of the treatment appears to reduce high muscle tone, ease constipation, improve vocalization prospects, reduce spasm and aid general relaxation (see the Useful Addresses and Contacts section).

## HANDLE therapy

HANDLEs therapy was devised by Judith Bluestone in the 1980s. Judith Bluestone had neurodevelopmental challenges as a child; this gave her the impetus to develop the HANDLE technique after 12 years of study in neuroscience, neuropsychology, neuro-rehabilitation, human development, visual processing, sensory-motor integration, education, counselling and more. She died in 2009 but her legacy lives on in the work of the HANDLE institute that she set up in 1994. She later received the Jefferson award for outstanding public services and the Jacqueline Kennedy award in 2004. More information is available on the HANDLE website (www.handle.org/). HANDLE embraces aspects of many other disciplines and therapies. Some of the theories and applications that HANDLE incorporates include:

- Montessori's educational concepts
- Kephart's visual-perceptual-motor programmes
- Ayres' sensory integration and praxis therapies
- the Bobaths' neurodevelopmental therapy
- Bates and Forrest's developmental optometry
- Tomatis and Berard's auditory therapies
- Irlen's scotopic sensitivity screening
- Piaget's cognitive psychology
- Werner's theories of development
- Doman-Delacato's theories of neurodevelopment and behaviour
- Lindamood's approach to language learning
- Fernauld's concepts of multisensory learning, and Slingerland's applications to reading
- Laban's theories of movement as language
- Umphred's philosophy on neurological rehabilitation.

HANDLE therapy also incorporates numerous other perspectives, including:

- the dynamics of social systems

- the significance of olfaction and other primary senses

- the effects of nutrition on neurodevelopment

- the theories behind homeopathy and reflexology

- concepts associated with myofascial release, cranio-sacral therapy and energy therapy.

The HANDLE programme is usually carried out in the home school setting. Small, measured doses of specific activities are incorporated into daily activities.

The recommended activities are simple to perform, and require virtually no special equipment. Each exercise programme is specially designed to meet the individual client's specific needs. Some of the more frequently suggested activities involve:

- rolling on the floor

- drinking through a crazy straw

- rhythmic hand bouncing

- being massaged by a rolling ball

- working in a dimly lit room.

Therapy time rarely exceeds 20 minutes daily, and usually the suggested activities can be performed as a sequence or broken into several clusters, depending upon individual preferences and schedules.

## Hyperbaric Oxygen Therapy

Hyperbaric Oxygen Therapy (HBO) is a medical treatment that uses 100 per cent oxygen to speed and enhance the body's natural ability to heal. It is given in a specially equipped, hyperbaric chamber that simulates being beneath sea level causing increased atmospheric pressure. The length of time in the chamber varies with each patient. The patient lies in a bed and is administered oxygen under these pressure conditions. It aims to reduce pressure within the brain caused by swelling, restoring function of the blood brain barriers and cell membranes. Recent research suggests that some improvement in motor function resulted from the use of HBO (Collet *et al.* 2001). It is possible to buy home chambers although they are expensive. A research study has supported HBO at: http://drcranton.com/hbo/hbo_proven_to_benefit_cp.htm and more advice can be sought at: http://www.advancecentres.com/hyperbaric_therapy.php.

# Chapter 5

# SPECIAL CONSIDERATIONS

## VACCINATION

Every child is likely to go through the usual round of childhood illnesses such as chicken pox, tummy upsets and the common cold. Previously common illnesses, such as measles, mumps and whooping cough, can be vaccinated against but some parents do not believe in vaccination. Children with cerebral palsy may appear to react more strongly than other children when they catch a commonplace illness. Commonplace illnesses can increase spasm, further inhibit control over movement and set back development – especially if during the illness the child's exercise programmes and other routines need to stop.

If your child is normally on an exercise programme which cannot be carried out due to illness, he will be likely to show signs of temporary deterioration in muscle control as well as the common symptoms associated with the illness. For this reason alone it is worth seriously considering having your child vaccinated against common complaints where a vaccination is available. It may be well worth your while to ensure that your child does not get held up by common illnesses any more than is necessary.

Some parents are concerned about dangerous side-effects from certain vaccinations. The whooping cough vaccination has particularly been highlighted as having potential dangers. These days even the whooping cough vaccination is recommended for virtually all children who have brain damage. It is also recommended that vulnerable children and the adults who care for them should have an annual flu jab.

## UNUSUAL SLEEP AND ATTENTION PATTERNS

I was frustrated to find that my experience of a sleepless, unhappy baby was not uncommon. Furthermore, I discovered that my son's constant constipation was also experienced by many of the children who have cerebral palsy. If someone had told me that these problems were associated with CP, and not due to my inadequate mothering, I might have cottoned on to remedial action a great deal sooner.

If your child is stiff, it is quite likely that he will get uncomfortable at night and wake more frequently than a baby who does not have disabilities. On the other hand, a floppy child or one who is taking barbiturates to control fits may seem lethargic and appear to be an overly 'good' baby. I have spoken to mothers who have been concerned about providing their baby with stimulation and play opportunities but have had difficulty waking their child up, and keeping them awake.

Many parents of children with CP notice that they cry a lot more than their siblings, or other children they have known. Other parents express concern that their baby just 'lies there' demonstrating no emotion. If a child is suffering discomfort as a result of his disability, it is no surprise that he expresses this in the only way a small child is able – by giving out distress signals through crying. If your child is extremely quiet and is also being administered drugs, it may be that the side-effects of the drugs are actually having a sedative effect which may impede his natural development process – although this is not necessarily always the case.

Whether your child cries a lot or is abnormally quiet, the natural learning process is being interfered with at an early stage. If you have a child who cries a lot, the first and most important priority is *not* to blame yourself. It is no reflection on your ability to cope or how good you are as a carer. Many children who have CP cry more than the average child.

Every family's experience is different but there is one need which all of our children have in common – a need to understand the world around them. The only way to be sure that they get the maximum opportunity for this is to offer them stimulation as often as possible which is appropriate to their age. In addition to this, a child who has restricted mobility needs help to gain access to the world through movement. If they cannot move by themselves we need to move them. If a small baby who has CP doesn't seem to notice you, this is all the more reason to make yourself noticeable. Wear bright colours and make sure there is plenty of light. If he does not seem to respond to sound, play him lots of music and make sure he hears lots of everyday sounds. If he does not move voluntarily, take his arms and legs and give them a chance to feel the world. If he seems very sensitive to touch, kiss and touch him a lot. This will have to be done gently but it is important that he overcomes any sensitivity of touch, so persevere. Eventually he will be able to tolerate touch and come to appreciate it.

There may be some alternative remedies which can aid sleep or stimulate action. These are discussed further in Chapter 8.

## COLDS AND CHEST INFECTIONS

Some children with CP may have a rather fast and shallow breathing rate and many are susceptible to colds and chest infections. Also, some children may find it difficult to cough up mucus either because they have an inefficient cough reflex or because the shallow breathing allows the mucus to lie on the chest.

There are various ways to deal with these problems. A physiotherapist may be able to suggest some exercises which will encourage deep breathing. Preventative action you can take using alternative methods is dealt with in Chapter 8. Conventional medicine tends to be geared towards treatment rather than prevention but there are a number of inhalers and drugs (antibiotics) which may be prescribed by your GP or consultant if your child gets a chest infection. You should not delay in getting treatment for your child if she has a chest infection. Antibiotics have a swift action and can stop an otherwise serious complication in its tracks. Even alternative practitioners will usually advise that you use conventional medicine such as antibiotics rather than risk your child becoming seriously ill with consequent interruption to her overall treatment. Antibiotics are not, however, effective for viral conditions.

Basic preventative action in the home includes ensuring your child is wrapped up warm if you are going out, keeping the atmosphere at home as dust free as possible, avoiding draughts in the home and maintaining a good diet high in vitamins and low on dairy produce (which tends to be mucus-forming).

## CONSTIPATION

Constipation can be one of the most incapacitating minor problems encountered by the young child or adult with CP. It is essential that you find a way to keep the bowels moving. If possible, methods should be found which will not further weaken or damage the intestinal tract. Strong laxatives are the worst for this and the child can become reliant on them. There are a number of readily available preparations which are made from natural substances that do not do permanent damage to the intestines. 'Fybrogel' is a good example and can be bought over the counter or obtained with a prescription from your GP or consultant. Preventative measures include close attention to diet, gentle massage (in a clockwise direction) on her tummy, just below the navel, at regular intervals and especially when she needs to go. There are a number of herbal preparations which can be given to help avoid constipation (see Chapter 8). Changes to diet may help. If all else fails, suppositories, which are glycerine based and comparatively harmless, will encourage bowel movement if your child is 'bunged up'. You should not administer suppositories as a matter of course but they can be used very effectively on an occasional basis without doing any long-term damage.

There may be certain foods you should avoid or could give more of to ease constipation. For example, roughage in the diet, plenty of fruit (especially plums or prunes), adding olive oil or ground sesame seeds or linseeds can all help. You may need to take care not to give your child too many dairy products as these can be binding. Ensure that your child gets sufficient liquid and drinks with her diet; a dietician can advise on the appropriate amounts.

## Recipe for easing constipation

The following recipe for easing constipation was given to me by a speech therapist. I have used it successfully with my own son and experienced a mixture of amusement and gratification when a parent I encountered at a conference loudly exclaimed 'You're the one who wrote the recipe for constipation aren't you? It did wonders for my daughter.'

INGREDIENTS

A 300 gram tin of prunes (stoned) plus the juice

Three large, ripe bananas

230 grams of mixed dried fruit (or 230 grams of dried apricots if preferred)

200 ml water

METHOD

Liquidize the ingredients and divide into ten portions which can be individually frozen. I would not recommend keeping the mixture in the fridge without freezing it. Either defrost on the appropriate microwave setting immediately before use or defrost overnight in the fridge before eating for breakfast.

The sauce can be put on breakfast cereals instead of (or as well as) milk, used as a drink, or offered as a pudding (if too thick to be used as a drink). You should begin by offering the child 15 ml per day of this recipe and work up to a regular consumption of 100 ml per day. Expect to wait up to a week for results. The recipe is sweet and very tasty.

## REFLUX

Reflux is very common in children with CP and is a severe form of acid indigestion. One of the stomach's jobs is to make acid; it helps us digest our food. The stomach lining is specially designed to resist damage from this acid, but the oesophagus, the food tube which extends from the back of the mouth to the stomach, is very sensitive to acid. Acid and stomach content do not normally flow back into the oesophagus. However, we have all experienced the sensation of 'reflux'. Stomach content may flow back into the oesophagus when we bend over, row a boat, lie down, or try to walk on our hands – any activity that puts pressure on the stomach or moves the oesophagus to a position that is lower than the stomach.

Refluxing is abnormal when it happens frequently, causes damage to our bodies, and interferes with our daily life. With gastroesophageal reflux disease (GERD), food and acid may spill into the windpipe and lungs, causing or worsening such pulmonary problems as asthma, bronchitis and pneumonia. When the oesophagus is irritated for long periods of time by acid reflux, it may form scar tissue and cause narrowing, producing a stricture, which makes it difficult to swallow food and even liquid. Some patients may experience more unusual symptoms such as throat pain, chronic cough or throat clearing, gagging, and sour taste in the mouth. There are various drug therapies available to try and combat the problems caused by reflux. In extreme cases surgical procedures such as gastrostomy may be suggested. Gastrostomy, a surgical procedure involving the creation of an opening into the stomach, enables nutrients to be delivered directly into the stomach.

## ASPIRATION

Aspiration is where small particles of food and/or drink enter the lungs. It could be due to a number of factors such as poor chewing skills, poor gag reflex (inability to cough up food that has gone down the wrong way) or incorrect positioning of the head while feeding. A physiotherapist can advise on positioning and a speech and language therapist can offer advice on the consistency of food and drink.

## OTITIS MEDIA (GLUE EAR)

Otitis media is a common, minor ailment which can affect disabled and non-disabled children alike. Many children without disability have been wrongly thought to have developmental delay because of this condition. It is an infection of the middle ear which may have a serious effect on the child's hearing due to the production of fluid 'glue' in the middle ear. It is slightly more common in pre-term infants than those born at term. Children who have CP may have long-term problems with hearing due to brain damage. On the other hand, otitis media can occur in addition to and quite separate from any brain damage, but have a further, unnecessary, disabling effect on the child. If you can't distinguish the sounds that are going on around you *and* you have restricted mobility, the situation could be very frustrating. It is already difficult enough to make your way through the developmental maze without the added complication of a curable infection. It is vitally important that you get your child's hearing checked regularly as otitis media is much more difficult to pick up in a child who has CP. There is sophisticated machinery available which can detect this condition fairly easily so that treatment can be rapidly administered. If the condition is severe it may require the insertion of grommets. Some parents and professionals believe that grommets should be inserted only as a last resort as they may increase the possibility of infection and prohibit certain activities such as swimming.

## SLOW GROWTH

A significant number of children who have cerebral palsy do not grow as quickly as non-disabled children of the same age. In many cases doctors are unable to explain this. However, two identifiable causes, 'failure to thrive' and growth hormone deficiency, are both treatable.

### Failure to thrive

Failure to thrive is a general term used by professionals to describe a child who is not growing properly, the cause of which may be poor nutrition. The classification is not specific to children who have cerebral palsy; many children who have no other disability are considered to be failing to thrive. There are a number of reasons why a child may appear to fail to thrive, particularly if the child has a severe physical disability.

Failure to thrive is sometimes assumed to be rooted in problems in the early relationship between mother and child. Emotional deprivation, physical neglect or abuse and withholding of food are commonly associated with this condition. It is also acknowledged in professional circles that the condition of cerebral palsy may, in itself, produce failure to thrive. Many children who have cerebral palsy have immense problems with the physical action required to eat. It may be very difficult to get the child to take in enough food to sustain him. Gastrostomy may be offered if this becomes an extreme problem.

The best advice that parents of children in this situation can be given is to ensure that the child receives a well-balanced, nutritious diet, and plenty of exercise to complement it. If feeding is so difficult that you cannot get your child to take in sufficient quantities you may wish to consider alternative ways of ensuring he receives enough nutrition. Your consultant should be able to help with this. A referral to a dietician as early as possible can help with sorting out the best, calorie-filled food to give your child which he can easily accept. I have found supplementing Dan's diet with concentrated protein drinks helpful (these are available from chemists). Also, adding banana or avocado and cream to the normal diet piles on the calories. If pressure on the family makes it difficult for the main carer to give the necessary time and attention to feeding, then social services should be contacted with a view to providing some help to carers. In practice this is by no means automatic and probably highly dependent on the area you live in.

### Growth hormone deficiency

Growth hormone deficiency is very rare. Sometimes there is brain damage which affects the mechanism which instructs the pituitary gland to release the growth hormone. There are tests which can be carried out for this (although it involves a number of blood tests and possible admission to hospital for a short period). If there is found to be a deficiency of growth hormone in the body there is an option to give growth hormone treatment.

## BEHAVIOURAL DISORDERS

In 2010 SIGURDARDOTTIR et al concluded that a large number of preschool children with CP have behavioural and emotional difficulties. Colver commented on the ways in which this study had affected his practice in that his assessments pay more attention to the pain experienced by children with CP and also with a focus on attention, sleep patterns, tantrums and how parents manage behaviour especially in the preschool years. He points out that the findings are broadly similar to older children with CP (Einarsdottir *et al.* 2010) There have been a number of studies since this that have similar findings (e.g. Humphrey 2006). Cause may differ from one individual to another and may not be connected to brain damage. The enormous pressures and stress put on the family and the child who has cerebral palsy may affect behaviour. There is often a lack of adequate counselling, information and practical assistance when it is immediately required in the early stages of discovering that a child has cerebral palsy. Comments from carers in my own survey suggest, overwhelmingly, that families feel unsupported and ill informed by the helping professions. The child may, understandably, feel frustrated by lack of mobility and muscular movements which refuse to obey the child's intention. It is difficult for parents to know exactly how to introduce the normal disciplines appropriate in child-rearing when they may be having difficulties understanding their child's communication and be distressed to witness their child's frustration. All of these things may contribute towards the development of behaviour disorders. The current medical thinking is that such disorders should be, as nearly as possible, treated in the same way as they would be in dealing with non-disabled children who have such problems.

Specific treatment for behaviour disorder will depend on its exact nature. There are basically three approaches available. The first one involves drug therapy, the second approach is behaviour modification using reward systems for appropriate behaviour and a third, less commonly available option is some form of psychotherapeutic counselling either for the carer, the child or the whole family. With this third option the family can together examine the problems that they are having and, with the help of a trained therapist, identify causes and explore solutions.

## HYPERACTIVITY

Hyperactivity means that the child is excessively physically active. In children with cerebral palsy this is often known as hyperkinesia, which describes the condition when the overactivity of the child is related to that child's development. The main characteristics are restlessness, impulsive behaviour, poor concentration span and difficulty in attending to what is being said or going on around them. On occasion, such children may be aggressive, anxious and poor eaters, have difficult sleeping patterns and experience social and learning difficulties. Children with this condition are not necessarily more active than the average child but their movements are likely to be less purposeful. Given the difficulty of interpreting the meaning of intentional movement in many children who have CP, the diagnosis of hyperkinesia is not an easy one to make.

There are a number of ways in which hyperactivity can be treated. A structured environment which includes plenty of time for relaxation may help. Overstimulation should be avoided (this is very difficult to achieve if your child has other difficulties calling for extra stimulation to help overcome them). Positive reinforcement (i.e. rewarding the child for behaviour which is calm and controlled) may help. There are drugs which can be used to control the effects of hyperactivity but they all have side-effects and these must be weighed up before administration, especially considering that a child with CP already has a number of other disabling experiences to grapple with and may require medication for these which might conflict with the medication prescribed for hyperactivity. These drugs modify the disturbances in attention span, concentration and impulsive behaviour. Side-effects of the drugs, in the short term, can include anorexia, abdominal pain, insomnia, drowsiness, headaches, nail biting, sensitivity and tearfulness. Long-term effects may include increased heart rate and growth suppression. Balancing the medication for hyperactivity is quite difficult and needs to be monitored carefully by your consultant.

It is very difficult to isolate hyperactivity as a specific problem relating to cerebral palsy. A restless and frustrated response to the world is quite understandable if you have a condition which makes it difficult for you to communicate or move in the way you want to. Consideration should be given to whether a child is exhibiting a natural reaction to a frustrating situation before hyperactivity is assumed.

## MICROCEPHALY

Microcephaly is a defect in the growth of the brain as a whole, and is caused by damage to the brain which restricts its ability to grow. The brain may be as much as 25 per cent underweight and it is possible that the frontal lobe will be the most severely affected, although this is variable. The forehead tends to slope markedly backwards and the ears may appear disproportionately large. Microcephaly tends to be associated with intellectual impairment. I can confirm, however, that I have taught a number of children who had microcephaly as part of their disability and who had normal intellectual function. Microcephaly must be distinguished from small head size, which is also common in children with cerebral palsy. There is no known treatment for microcephaly.

## HYDROCEPHALY

Hydrocephaly is a build-up (beyond the normal) of the cerebrospinal fluid within the skull. The main symptom is usually a gradual increase in the size of the upper part of the head out of proportion to the face or the rest of the body. Hydrocephalus has historically been associated with birth fatality or low intellectual progress. However, treatment has become much more successful over recent years. The most common treatment is to implant a valve (known as a shunt) which drains off excess fluid. The problem with the implanting of shunts is that they can cause infection, or may become blocked, and further exacerbate the condition.

## EPILEPSY

There are different types of epilepsy which are of varying severity and effect. Up to half of the children who have cerebral palsy are likely to have one type of seizure or another, either on an occasional basis or at regular intervals. Epilepsy is a common condition irrespective of other brain damage and it is thought to affect up to 290,000 people in England and Wales alone; it affects 3 million Americans and 50 million people worldwide. A seizure (or 'fit' as they used to be known) is caused by a temporary change in the way the brain cells work. When a child has a seizure, an upset in brain chemistry causes the messages to become scrambled. When this happens the neurons in the brain fire off faster than usual, triggering off a seizure.

### Types of epileptic seizures

SIMPLE PARTIAL SEIZURES (WITHOUT IMPAIRMENT OF CONSCIOUSNESS)

Simple partial seizures occur in just part of the brain. The symptoms depend on the area of the brain involved and could include one or more of the following: twitching, numbness, sweating, dizziness, nausea, disturbances to hearing, vision, smell or taste, etc. These symptoms last for several seconds and then go away. The person remains fully aware. These seizures can progress to other types of seizure and can therefore act as a warning sign.

COMPLEX PARTIAL SEIZURES (WITH IMPAIRMENT OF CONSCIOUSNESS)

Complex partial seizures are a common form of seizure and can lead to strange automated behaviour, such as plucking at clothes, smacking lips, swallowing repeatedly or wandering around as if drunk. Other symptoms are similar to simple partial seizures but the person may not remember them afterwards. The person is not aware of their surroundings or of what they are doing.

### ABSENCE SEIZURES

Absence seizures used to be called 'Petit Mal'. The person has a momentary lapse in awareness and stops what they are doing, stare, blink or look vague for a few seconds before carrying on with what they were doing. Onlookers may think the person is just daydreaming or may not notice.

### MYOCLONIC SEIZURES

Myoclonic seizures are usually brief and involve shock-like jerks caused by rapidly alternating contraction and relaxation of muscles. They also include atonic seizures (drop attacks).

### TONIC-CLONIC SEIZURES

Tonic-clonic seizures are the most common sort of generalized seizure. They used to be called 'Grand Mal'. In the tonic phase the muscles contract, the body stiffens and then the clonic phase occurs with uncontrollable jerks. The person may let out a cry as air is forced out of the lungs and the lips may go blue due to lack of oxygen. The person loses consciousness and when they come round they cannot remember anything. It can take anything from minutes to hours to recover from this type of seizure.

### UNCLASSIFIED SEIZURES

All the seizures that are not fully understood and don't fit into any of the above categories are known as unclassified seizures. They include symptoms such as rhythmic eye movements, chewing and swimming movements.

## Diagnosis and treatment of epilepsy

Diagnosis of the type of fit your child is experiencing is usually obtained through electroencephalography (EEG). This is carried out by a machine recording the spontaneous electrical activity in the brain by placing electrodes on specific points on the scalp and electronically recording events in the cortical and sub-cortical areas of the brain. Different types of epilepsy tend to produce recognizable wave patterns.

## DRUG THERAPY

There are a number of instances where drug therapy may be offered to children (and adults) who have cerebral palsy. Most common are those offered to control convulsions and those for relief of tensions and muscle spasm. In addition drugs may be offered to relieve constipation, help with sleep, reduce anxiety, reduce hyperactivity and to ease pain after operations. Great care must be taken when the decision to offer drugs is made. It is necessary to ensure that the dose is right, that it can be maintained within safe limits and also that there are no other preparations on prescription which might adversely interact with what is being proposed.

## Drugs used to control seizures (anticonvulsants)

Any general depressant of the nervous system will decrease or abolish epileptic fits but the ones used to treat epilepsy have been selected because they reduce excessive stimulation in the brain without depressing viral centres (such as the respiratory centre) and without sending the patient to sleep. The cause and type of epilepsy must be established before treatment is offered. The selection of the most appropriate drug and dosage is critical and it may take several months to get a patient's symptoms controlled on a particular drug. It is essential that patients follow instructions for taking these drugs exactly and adverse side-effects should be noted and reported to the prescribing doctor.

The dose of an anti-convulsant drug often needs to be slowly increased over time as the body builds up tolerance. This means that the drug becomes ineffective as the body gets used to it. Unfortunately the level of the drug in the system which is toxic does not change. This means that the higher the dose is increased the nearer the patient gets to having toxic levels of the drug in his system. When this happens the patient may have to be switched to another anti-convulsant. The changeover must be carried out very slowly, as should withdrawal or decreasing the levels of drugs. This is because sudden withdrawal of anti-convulsants can have marked and dangerous effects, which may include anxiety, restlessness, trembling, weakness, abdominal cramps, vomiting, hallucinations, delirium, fits and even death.

Driving and operating machinery needs to be avoided if the patient develops drowsiness as a result of taking these drugs. Some anti-convulsant drugs reduce the effectiveness of oral contraception and there is a slight risk of abnormalities being produced in babies if taken during pregnancy. Frequent blood level monitoring should be carried out at the beginning of treatment until the patient is stabilized. Children require more regular and higher dosing than adults as they break down the drugs more quickly. Multiple drug therapy (combining more than one anti-convulsant) should be considered very carefully as this further complicates monitoring and increases the risk of adverse side-effects from the interaction of drugs. The effects of alcohol combined with the effects of anti-convulsant drugs can sometimes be dangerous.

## Drugs used as muscle relaxants

Care must be taken when administering muscle relaxants to take account of any other regular drug use (such as anti-convulsants) as there is a high possibility of muscle relaxant drugs contradicting other drugs.

Diazepam (Valium) is a popular muscle relaxant. Baclofen (Lioresal) is also widely used. Intra Thecal Baclofen is being used in some hospitals as a way of reducing side-effects and making the delivery of Baclofen more controllable. This involves infusing the spinal fluid with Baclofen via a drip feed through a pump at a slow rate. Dantrolene sodium (Dantrium) used to be popular but its use is gradually diminishing.

## Drugs and their side-effects

The side effects of anticonvulsant and muscle relaxing drugs are impossible to predict on an individual basis but can include a number of symptoms such as:

- drowsiness

- nausea

- dizziness

- fatigue

- stomach upset

- confusion

- mood change

- change in appetite

- rashes

- depression

- restlessness

- insomnia

- increased seizures.

If your child begins to show any of the above signs after starting on a course of drug therapy you should inform your GP or the consultant. Information about antiepileptic drugs can be found at www.epilepsy.org.uk/info/treatment/uk-anti-epileptic-drugs-list and www.epilepsyfoundation.org/aboutepilepsy/treatment/medications/index.cfm.

## Drugs used to decrease anxiety

Diazepam (Valium) and related drugs are those principally used to treat anxiety. Diazepam belongs to the chlordiazepoxide drug family which has four properties: sedative, anti-anxiety, muscle relaxant and anti-convulsant.

## Drugs used to aid sleep

Drugs in this group depress brain function; in smaller doses they are used as sedatives (to calm patients down) and in larger doses as hypnotics (to send patients to sleep). They are all habit forming so that patients may quickly become dependent on them. This can be made worse by an increase in restlessness at night when the drug is withdrawn. Tolerance can develop and the side-effects may include anxiety, irritability and depression. They should not be mixed with alcohol. They may impair learning, affect concentration and produce confusion.

## Drugs used to control hyperactivity

Stimulants are used to control hyperactivity. These drugs and their side-effects are discussed in the previous section on hyperactivity.

## Drugs used to ease constipation

Drugs that ease constipation are called laxatives and care must be taken not to use them too regularly. They should never be taken to relieve abdominal pains, cramps, colic, nausea or any other symptoms even if these are associated with constipation.

A high fibre diet, with plenty of fluids, is the most natural way to treat constipation. This is achieved by eating more fruit and leafy vegetables and by adding bran to the diet.

There are many preparations on the market but there are four main categories of laxative:

- stimulant laxatives (bisacodyl, cascara, castor oil, danthron, fig, senna, sodium picosulphate)

- saline laxatives (magnesium sulphate, magnesium hydroxide, sodium sulphate, sodium potassium tartrate, potassium bitrate, lactulose)

- lubricant laxatives (mineral oils, diotyl sodium sulphosuccinate, poloxamer)

- bulk forming laxatives (agar, tragacanth, ispaghula husks, sterculia, bran).

Stimulant laxatives increase large bowel movement by irritating the lining and/or stimulating the bowel muscles to contract. They may cause cramps, increased mucus secretion and excessive fluid loss. Side-effects vary enormously from person to person.

Saline laxatives increase the bulk of the bowel by causing it to retain water. They take fluids from the body and can cause dehydration, and should therefore be taken with large drinks of water. Lactulose may cause nausea, diarrhoea and wind.

Lubricant laxatives soften the faeces. Mineral oils such as liquid paraffin should be used with extreme caution as they interfere with the absorption of vitamin A and vitamin D and can be dangerous if accidentally inhaled.

Bulk forming laxatives increase the bulk content of the bowel which stimulates the bowel to become active. They must be taken with plenty of fluids to avoid the risk of bowel obstruction.

When faeces are impacted, laxatives administered rectally may be useful. A number of preparations are available, the most harmless of which are probably glycerol suppositories.

## Drugs administered post-operatively

The main drugs used during a hospital stay involving any kind of operation are analgesias or muscle relaxants to relieve pain. Among the most commonly used are pethidine, morphine, diazepam (Valium) and Narcan. As with many other drugs, care must be taken to take account of any long-term drugs the patient is on in case there are contraindications of their use together with particular analgesias.

## Alternatives to drug therapy

Alternatives exist for all drug therapy but patients and parents should be careful about turning to other possible treatments. It would be extremely unwise and potentially dangerous, for example, suddenly to take a child who has epilepsy off anti-convulsant drugs because you believe you have discovered a herbal alternative. If you want to try an alternative you should ensure that it is under the guidance of a well-qualified alternative practitioner and that you discuss slow reduction of anti-convulsants with your doctor first. Alternative practitioners may well advise that you maintain your child on anti-convulsant drugs but that they might be able to help you to keep the dosage at a low level by complementing drug therapy. Also, some alternative treatments have adverse side-effects, although they are unlikely to be as severe as those experienced under conventional drug therapy. Complementary and alternative treatments are discussed in some detail in Chapter 8.

Chapter 6

# ALTERNATIVES TO VERBAL COMMUNICATION

A number of specialists can be expected to become involved if the child is likely to have communication difficulty. The speech and language therapist may advise on receptive language understanding (as may the psychologist) and alternatives to speech. The occupational therapist and/or clinical technician may offer advice on positioning and access to communication aids. The doctor or consultant may make a referral to a communication aid centre. A social worker might become involved in helping you to obtain funding for a communication aid.

## AUGMENTATIVE AND ALTERNATIVE COMMUNICATION

AAC complements or supports speech. A person might have some speech but is not able to say as much as they want to and so can supplement their communication with AAC. They might sign or they might use a communication book or an alphabet board. They might also use a high tech device which speaks out loud. 'Alternative' means instead of speech. AAC can sometimes be used when a person is unable to write or type using an ordinary computer. It can also be used to help a person who has learning difficulties to understand situations better and/or to learn better.

### Expressive and receptive communication

There are two distinct types of communication that can be supported by AAC: expressive and receptive communication.

- *Expressive communication* is the act of transmitting information or ideas. Speaking to someone, giving a talk, writing something for others to read and pointing to your choice out of a set of options are all examples of expressive communication.

- *Receptive communication* is the act of receiving communication. Listening to someone, reading and recognizing another person's choice are all examples of receptive communication.

## NO TECH AAC

No tech or unaided AAC involves using the body to communicate. It might be through sign language or less complex signs such as a nod, a shake of the head or a gesture. Children with CP who have communication difficulties often develop their own sign systems based on movements that they can manage. It is important to try to understand the meaning of these signs so that two-way communication can be established. If the child can be encouraged to develop a way of indicating YES and NO, it will enable you to establish the meaning of other signs. If all the child can do is indicate YES and NO, this is an excellent starting point. You have to be careful to ask closed questions. For example, if you want to know where the child wants to go you should phrase the question as follows:

> I'm going to give you four options. Listen to them first. Would you like to go to the park, the cinema, the bowling alley or somewhere else? The park [pause for a YES or NO answer], the cinema [pause for a YES or NO answer], the bowling alley [pause for a YES or NO answer], somewhere else? [pause for a YES or NO answer].

If the last answer is chosen you would need to think of three other options and so on.

The age at which children are normally able to communicate effectively with YES and NO is between 9 and 18 months. NO is normally the first to be understood (between 9 and 12 months) and understanding YES can come considerably later. If this ability does not seem to be developing naturally, I would suggest that it is actively introduced at the appropriate age.

An earlier language skill is the ability to indicate STOP or FINISH and MORE. Most children will engage with non-verbal behaviour to indicate that they have had enough from a very early age and certainly by nine months. They will also have non-verbal ways to indicate that they want more, often by reaching out for a desired object. Verbalization of 'more' will often follow modelling by the caregiver. Your speech and language therapist may encourage you to develop the MORE and STOP skills and get them established before the YES and NO skill. Other therapists would suggest tackling both together if the age of the child is appropriate for both skills. I would agree with this latter approach. It is not always easy to establish the level of understanding of a person who has not yet established communication, so an optimistic presumption would make sense rather than holding a person back with a pessimistic presumption. If the person doesn't understand, it will become clearer through trying an activity than ignoring it in case.

Formal sign language or a modified form such as Makaton may help the development of receptive language where learning difficulties occur. They may not, however, be appropriate frontline expressive language approaches for children who have fine motor difficulties. Makaton is also available as a symbols system.

## LOW TECH AAC

Low tech refers to the use of paper, cardboard, plastic or other materials on to which words, photographs, pictures, symbols, raised textures or small objects can be mounted so that the person who is wishing to communicate can point to them or indicate which one they want with assisted scanning. Low tech AAC can be used for many different purposes.

### Books for communication

Books for communication can be created by parents. They might have an index page and then individual topic pages to help with communication. For example the index page might have category headings such as 'Social', 'I need help', 'Food', 'Drink', 'People', 'Places to go', etc. If the owner of the book points to 'Places to go', their communication partner will navigate to the appropriate page which will have a range of places on it that the person might like to visit.

### Books for learning

Books for learning can also be created by parents. They might have an index page and then individual topic pages to help with learning. The index page would have subjects on it or topic areas such as school subjects, for example biology, physics, chemistry, geography etc. You might have further index or topic pages within a subject area. So, for example, a set of geography pages might include pages on geographical topics as shown in the illustration.

I sometimes make this kind of book using word tables, inserting photographs to illustrate the words. You don't need to buy expensive equipment and software to be able to make a communication book, especially since the emergence of Google and other image banks on the internet.

There is debate about whether words should be below pictures or above them. From a teaching point of view it is conventional to have pictures above the words, but from an access point of view it might be better to have the words above the pictures because you obscure the word when you point. Always include the word even if you don't think the child can read. Exposure to text may help reading skills to develop.

I have made communication books for people who index finger point, fist point, use a head pointer or eye point and you need a different layout for each. Layout is very important. If someone needs to fist point or has difficulty with accuracy, I would have less on a page and space the options out more. I work with a number of people who can only manage a few options on a page. In this case you have to be very creative about the options you put there so that they can indicate that what they want isn't there. It is essential to have a way of indicating that your choice isn't there on any page that could have more options than the ones given. The four corners of a page are not the easiest to access for many people. A North South East West arrangement is often better. For some AAC users it is best to arrange options in a zigzag pattern. This allows you to maximize what is on the page with space around each option to allow for movement error.

There are a number of different software options available for making communication and learning books or boards.

These include:

- Boardmaker: www.mayer-johnson.co.uk/boardmaker-v-6-uk-edition/

- Grid 2: www.sensorysoftware.com/thegrid2.html

- Communicate in Print: www.widgit.com/products/inprint/index. htm

- Mind Express 4: www.techcess.co.uk/4_6_Mind-Express-4.php

- Communicator 4: www.tobii.com/en/assistive-technology/global/ products/software/tobii-communicator/

- Matrix Maker: www.inclusive.co.uk/matrix-maker-p4837

It is also possible to use freely available symbol systems along with word tables or PowerPoint such as Mulberry: straight-street.com/gallery.php

The less you have in a set of options, the more difficult it is to be specific about the choices. If you were using the four on a page option you might need to have a set of four for hot drinks, and another for cold drinks, etc.

with possibly a 'more' selection on each one. For people who need to eye point, I place the options round the outside and cut a hole in the middle so that I can watch their eye movements from the other side of the page. It's a good idea to make sure that you have the choices written on your side as well so you know immediately what they are looking at. If someone is using a board or book for the first time, make sure you give them time to look at the options before you ask them to make a choice. Give a clear indication about when you want the person to make a choice (once they appear to have scanned all the options). If you are using an eye pointing board, you can ask them to look back at you when they have made their choice to confirm their choice, although this isn't always necessary. One tip for making an eye pointing book is to buy a display book (available at most stationery outlets) to place pages in. You need to check that the plastic inserts are clear and easy to see through.

Symbol systems are sets of pictures (usually line drawings) that have been developed for use with people who need to point to options to communicate and who have not yet developed full literacy. The commonly used symbol systems include the Widgit Literacy Symbol system, the Bliss symbolic system, Symbol Stix, Makaton and the Mayer Johnson Picture Communication Symbols (PCS). If you would rather not make your own communication boards or books, there are a number of pre-made systems that can be purchased for various ages and stages. Your local communication aid centre should be able to help you identify an appropriate choice.

*Figure 6.1 It is important to plan the layout communication
pages to meet the needs of the person.*

## Talking Mats

Talking Mats is a low tech system which uses symbols. It was designed by AAC
Scotland at the University of Stirling. Talking Mats aims to help people who
have significant communication difficulty to arrive at decisions by assigning
options along a continuum from very positive to very negative. You can find
out more at their website www.talkingmats.com or by contacting them at
the address in the Useful Addresses and Contacts section. Talking Mats has

been used by people with a wide range of needs and ages including people with cerebral palsy and people with dementia.

## Creating communication charts for adults

Adults with communication difficulties are in a different situation from young learners. They are no longer in the age group where learning new skills is automatically expected of them. If they have previously not been able to demonstrate communication skills, it may be difficult for them to find the motivation to try even if you offer them a new opportunity. If they have previously been assessed over a number of years as having little understanding they might not even be offered new opportunities as they arise. In addition to all this, many adults with communication difficulties will have been placed in environments where their needs have for a long while been anticipated by those who have been around them for a long time. They may have even become comfortable with this and could resist attempts to change their circumstances, even when you think it is in their interest.

For these reasons it is important that you take time introducing AAC and do not make the experience stressful for the adult. Here are some tips:

- Try to find out what the person really enjoys and offer them choices out of a group of options which will all be well received. This is called 'error free choice making'. An adult might need to continue with this kind of selection for much longer than a younger person might have done.

- Do not 'value judge' what a person enjoys. If a positive choice is to sit for an hour with a particular 'fiddle' activity, that is the person's choice and it should be respected.

- Don't test them to see if they can prove that they understand. Whether or not the person understands, they may have many years of 'failed' testing behind them and to test them is only likely to make them resist the opportunity you want to give them.

- Many people with communication difficulties have more understanding than they can demonstrate. They may not be able to speak and they seem to point randomly. This may be because they have hitherto undetected motor issues which make pointing difficult. Appropriate physical support to access a communication aid in the early days might help. The key to success in this situation is to stay respectful and to treat the person as if they have the same understanding that you do.

- If you are using a daily schedule with an adult, it needs to be handled carefully. Respect is essential. If the person is not able to immediately identify the next activity on their schedule line, you do it for them as a model without making them feel that they have failed.

- A really supportive option is for the person to have a support circle of people who agree to help them to achieve their personal goals. It may be that, in the early stages, the group's focus is to help the person to identify those goals. The group do not have to be personal friends. They just need to be people who would like to help.

- There is an older generation of people with learning difficulties who have missed out on the early opportunities now available to young people thanks to the advances in information technology. It is essential that this group get access to some of the opportunities that information technology offers. At the very least there should be access to choice making with voice output (communication aids that speak). They don't all have to be expensive.

- Don't try to use communication boards to teach grammar unless the adult wants you to. Functional communication (getting your message across) is more important. Single word requests are fine and do not reflect the word level understanding of the person.

- Initially, you may need to use communication charts that will have tangible results such as requests. People are less likely to start using social chat boards or even feelings pages until they have become confident with request boards. If a person has only physical difficulties and no learning difficulties, the situation may be different and a wide range of boards can be introduced according to their wishes.

## Using PowerPoint for making communication boards, charts and learning aids

PowerPoint is a very powerful tool that comes with Microsoft Office. It was originally designed to support business people and educators to give presentations using data projector technology so that they could throw an image onto a screen. It superseded the old acetate we used to draw and type onto and then project using an overhead projector. PowerPoint allows you to import photographs, clip art and video. You can record your voice on it which can be associated with an image. You can also place text anywhere on the page and create links to programmes which will open when you click on the link. In short, PowerPoint can be made to do virtually anything that most special needs software can do but you have to work a bit harder. I have used PowerPoint to make eye pointing books, communication books and boards, and even to create high tech communication and learning resources. There are detailed instructions on how to make PowerPoint communication and learning aids on this website: http://candleacc.com/using_powerpoint.htm

## Using specialized software for making communication boards, books and learning aids

The best known software designed for making communication pages are Boardmaker and Communicate in Print, both of which are available from Widgit at www.widgit.com (see Figure 6.2). I also use Grid 2 for making pages although Grid 2 is primarily designed for use with high tech machines. This is available from Sensory Software at www.sensorysoftware.com. There are several symbol systems that can be used with these software packages and you can also import your own pictures or just use text. If you are only using text a word table is adequate for your needs. Symbol systems include: Widgit Literacy Symbols, Mayer-Johnson PCS at www.mayer-johnson.co.uk, Symbolstix at symbolstix.n2y.com, Makaton and Blissymbolics at www.blissymbolics.org/pfw. The software enables you to design pages to your own access needs. Communicate in Print is also symbol supported desktop publishing which can be used for making symbol supported worksheets. For details of software contacts see the Useful Addresses and Contacts section.

## Low tech alphabet charts and pages

Spelling charts are quite a complex science all of their own. You can design them to look like a normal computer keyboard (QWERTY) for the person who is used to that layout. Some people prefer an alphabetic layout and for others frequency of use (most commonly used letters in the easiest to access place). At CandLE we provide a waterproof, high contrast, durable spelling board in QWERTY layout which can be found at www.contactcandle.co.uk/sales.htm and there is also a downloadable letter board in either QWERTY or alphabetical order that you can download and laminate at www.contactcandle.co.uk/downloads.htm. There are also some useful eye pointing pages and other resources available at this link. Another high contrast board is available from www.fab.uk.com which is spill proof but not totally waterproof.

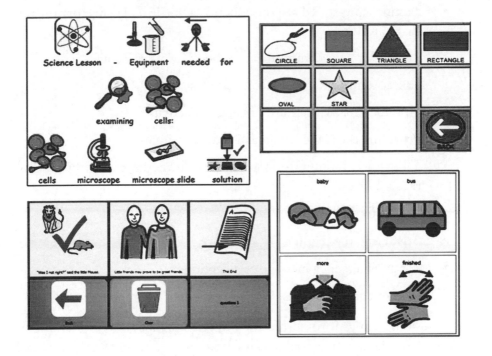

*Figure 6.2 Symbol writing software. Top left: Communicate in Print.*
*Top right: Communicator 4. Bottom left: Grid 2. Bottom Right: Boardmaker.*

## LIGHT TECH AAC

Otherwise known as basic high tech, light tech refers to devices that are relatively inexpensive and have a limited number of buttons on them. Pressing the button will trigger a word or a phrase to be spoken out loud by the device. There is usually a way of recording someone's voice onto these devices. This is known as digitized speech. There is a very wide range of light tech devices available.

### Single message communication aids

The most commonly known light tech device is a Big Mack (nothing to do with a popular fast food chain). The Big Mack is a large, round disc rather like a huge mouse that you press to activate a pre-recorded message. For a single message device it is quite expensive but it is fairly robust. There are many uses for a Big Mack, or other single message communication devices, but it is not useful for indicating a choice or for interaction that is two way. Uses for a Big Mack include:

- Timing a pre-stored response such as a line in a play or story during shared reading.

- Asking for your communication book or other device.

- Taking a message for someone else.

- To indicate that you have finished an activity.

- Providing the choice in an assisted scan situation.

- Telling a communication partner to 'turn the page' when being read a story.

- Asking for help.

- Answering the register.

- For an emergency message by telephone.

- Home school messages.

There are some things I would not use a single message for. For example, if you only have the message 'read it again' how are you going to indicate 'read something different' or 'I don't want to hear any more stories'.

You can find suggestions by putting 'ways to use a Big Mack' in a search engine on the internet. Other single message communicators include Talking Tins, Chipper, Go Talk Button, Go Talk Card (which lets you put a picture and a talking message on a greetings card), Go Talk One, One Talk and Viosec.

## Step by step communication aids

Step by step communication aids look like single message communication aids but will store a number of consecutive message so that it says something different every time you press it. There are a number of uses that these devices can have including:

- a part in a play

- a set of instructions to remind someone who has learning difficulties of an important sequence in daily living

- practising social situations with a communication partner.

A step by step communication aid doesn't help you to make choices or freely interact but can be very useful for instructions and for helping you to say things that are completely predictable. There are a number of step by step devices including Little Step, 'Little Step with levels' (which lets you specify the sequence you want) and Sequencer. A Randomizer plays back pre-recorded messages in random order and is very useful as an alternative dice for making other random choices.

## Communication aids with two options

Communication aids with two options offer some choice making and can help you to set up a situation where a person can use YES and NO to communicate using careful closed questioning or assisted scan. You can also record two choices such as 'more' and 'stop' for a younger child to join in with a game. Except for the possibility of giving someone the opportunity to say YES and NO the two switch option is still a little limiting, especially as there is no way of giving them the option to say 'none of these'. Two option communication aids include iTalk2 and Twintalker.

## Communication aids with four options

If you have four options you begin to have the option for the person to tell you their choice isn't there but you still have to think carefully about the purpose of the communication you are offering them access to and which choices will be the best to give them. Here are some examples of four choices that might be useful:

- Quick responses
  - Yes, no, I don't know, maybe.
  - Yes, no, I'm not sure, I don't care.
  - Yes, no, I can't decide, yes and no.
  - Yes, no, you choose, I don't want to do anything.
  - How are you?, I'm fine, Things are not so good, I've not been well.
- Coding
  - 1, 2, 3, 4 (you can have 16 options on a more complex board or device and the person can indicate the column and row like grid referencing a map).
  - A, B, C, D (you can use letters instead of numbers for grid referencing and also to support the curriculum: I have often assigned a set of possible answers this way in multiple choice so that I don't need to keep writing out all the choices).
  - Yellow, blue, green, red (colours can be used in the same way as numbers and letters). It is even possible to use colour coding

to spell but you need to use three hits for each letter so it only works well if you are spelling in a context that is known by your communication partner so that they can guess at the words for you to say yes or no.

- Making a choice when there is a limited range available
  - o Banana, apple, raisins, nothing thanks.
  - o Orange juice, apple juice, milk, water.
  - o Bowling, cinema, pub, stay home.
  - o Chicken, lamb, beef, another meat.
  - o Chicken, lamb, beef, more options.

## Using light tech devices with increased range and levels

There are a wide variety of light tech devices that have more than four options. Some have interchangeable templates so that the AAC user can choose from a range of options. Some also have levels which means that you can change the options either by flicking a switch or by placing an insert into the machine which triggers the device. Examples of devices include:

- *Super Talker* offers a choice of one to eight selections with eight levels. This means that a maximum of 64 options can be accessed.

- *Voicepal 8k* is an eight option device without levels.

- *Voicepal Levels* offers a choice of between two and ten selections with four levels. This means a maximum of 40 options can be accessed.

- *Talara-32* offers between 2 and 32 options on four levels.

- *Go-Talk 9+ and Go-Talk 20+* are very lightweight devices with a handle that have five levels and a small section for additional core vocabulary.

- *Voice Cue* can record up to five reminders that will speak at the appropriate time to remind the user to, for example, take their medicine.

- *MegaBee* is a light tech eye pointing alphabet which displays the items that have been eye pointed to on a screen. The text can then be transferred to a word processing document if desired.

- *Rotary Indicator* is a board rather like a clock face which can have words, pictures, drawings or objects placed on it. An arm then slowly spins round until it is pointing to the choice which is selected by pressing a switch.

- *The Amdi series* is available from QED offering a wide range of selection options as well as levels. Selection could be as little as two on a page or as many as 32 or even more. Levels refers to the ability to have a number of different choices on one button that can be changed by putting a new template on to the page (see the Useful Addresses and Contacts section).

Some of these light tech aids are shown in Figure 6.3.

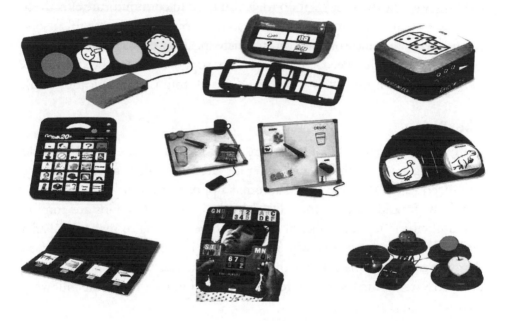

*Figure 6.3 Examples of light tech aids. Left to right top: Scan Talker, Super Talker, Randomizer. Left to right middle: Go-Talk 20+, Rotary Indicator, italk2. Left to right bottom: Talk Book 4, MegaBee, Take N' Talk.*

## HIGH TECH AAC

Technology is changing all the time so this is the area where information will go out of date very quickly. It is advisable to keep an eye on some of the online advice which is updated regularly. There is a list of these at the end of this section. These devices are usually very sophisticated. There are a number of suppliers that sell and support these devices. Many of these devices have dynamic screens. This means that you can press an area on the screen (often a cell that looks like a square) and you will automatically be taken to another page of options. Other high tech devices may rely on spelling and have a keyboard as their main input. The voice is usually electronic. This is known as synthesized speech. There is often a facility to record your own voice on to them as well. With the rapid change in technology it would be impossible, in a publication like this one, to provide you with up to date information on devices, because anything I write about today will probably have been superseded by a more compact and powerful alternative even before this book goes to print. However, the specifications of a computer are less important than the software that makes it do what you need to communicate effectively and the way in which you will access it so that you can be successful.

A device that has software on it which speaks a message out loud and enables people who need communication support to express themselves more effectively is known as a VOCA (Voice Output Communication Aid).

## The iPad

Many practitioners and families where AAC is needed have hailed the iPad as breaking new ground in providing an affordable alternative for people who need AAC. In reality the iPad offers opportunities for a relatively few people who need voice output but more and more AAC apps are coming out all the time and a number of companies are working to make the iPad a viable alternative for people who need AAC. It is really important, however, that you carefully consider how the person will access the iPad and what the best software is. Three good sources of information for this are the following websites:

- AppsFor AAC: www.appsforaac.net/

- NetBuddy: www.netbuddy.org.uk/info-packs/apps-ipad

- CandLE: www.candleaac.com/advice_on_iPad_and_iPod_apps.htm

## Keyboard based devices

Keyboard based devices have a keyboard and the facility to speak out what you type but they do not have symbol-supported options or dynamic screen.

## Dedicated communication devices

Dedicated devices have been created with the intention of providing voice output communication. This means that they speak out loud as you choose an option by pressing it on a touch screen or selecting it by other means such as switches or a mouse or joystick. These devices are becoming less popular as a new technology which allows devices to be both communication aids and fully functioning computers is developing. Some dedicated devices are hand held, which are useful for mobile AAC users who have good fine motor skills.

## Minspeak

One piece of software that is often sold with dedicated communication devices is Minspeak. This is a language that has been developed for the communication aid user who has a very good grasp of language and memory skills. The developers have also designed simpler devices to support those who are learning to use communication aids. The most sophisticated version has 144 keys with representative symbols that are pressed in various combinations to produce communication at a complex level. Many thousands of words can be generated by various combinations of the keys and it is possible to add to this with the use of a spelling page. This is a very good system for someone who can learn it. It is complicated to learn but quick for those who know how to use it. I have a friend who uses this system and she is one of the fastest AAC users I know.

Liberator is a UK company that produces a range of devices which support Minspeak. Prentke Romich Company do the same in the USA. They support a number of language programmes including a basic one called 'Teach and Talk' which is aimed at students working within P levels. Built into 'Teach and Talk' is the potential to begin basic Minspeak training once a student reaches a certain level of proficiency.

## Computers as communication devices

Computers that use specialist software are useful and accessible for AAC users. At the time of writing this type of high tech aid is increasing in popularity. Many of these computers being used are touch screen. There was a time that touch screens were very rare and expensive but thanks to a commercial interest in the technology from the retail trade, those that run utilities and the health service, they are becoming more and more commonplace. This means that the technology should theoretically become cheaper.

A touch screen is not as simple as it may sound. It means that you can touch the screen at the place where you want to activate something when you would usually use a mouse. Some touch screens only respond to an electronic pen and others only respond to a metal stylus. The only touch screens that are useful for AAC users also respond to fingertip touch (often known as dual control) so you need to be sure that you choose your touch screen computer carefully.

One advantage of computer based devices is that you can mix and match the software that you put on it. You might prefer the device that one company provides but the software might be supplied from elsewhere. You also have the option to go out and purchase a touch screen computer in the high street and put the software on yourself. However, suppliers do produce casing for computers that will often contain amplifiers to increase the volume and extra battery life so that you can use them all day without needing to recharge them. Suppliers may also agree to be responsible if anything goes wrong in the first year or so.

## Eye gaze technology

There has been a recent upsurge of interest in eye gaze technology, which uses cameras that can read your eye movements and directional gaze so that you can trigger options just by looking at them. It isn't as easy as it sounds to operate an eye gaze device. You need to be able to control eye movements to a certain extent and you must be able to calibrate the machine so that it 'learns' your eye movements. Once you have achieved this, you need to keep your energy levels (not to mention your head) up for talking by looking. In my experience people who cannot talk instinctively use their hands/fingers to point and then turn to directional gaze if they are additionally unable to use their hands. So eye gaze is not a natural frontline access strategy. It is, however, offering wonderful opportunities to people who have been unable to express themselves by pointing and have trouble with joysticks and switches. Eye gaze is currently very expensive. I have spent months and even years preparing students for being ready to access eye gaze technology by encouraging them to practise using low tech equivalents.

The Cogain project has extensive information about eye gaze: see www.cogain.org/

## Hand held devices

Small hand held devices that are compatible with a computer are alternatively known as personal digital assistants (PDAs) and palm top computers. Although they are too small to have full Windows capacity, they can be configured to carry out most of the functions of a normal computer. A number of companies have developed software for a range of devices which they sell as specialist hand held AAC devices.

## Vocabularies

There have been a number of vocabularies produced which can usually be used in conjunction with most software. Vocabularies are sets of dynamic pages which attempt to enable a person to use pre-prepared pages to communicate rather than having to write them from scratch.

# ACCESS OPTIONS FOR AAC

AAC offers wonderful opportunities to people who may have struggled with communication and learning but it is not a simple matter of just going out and buying a communication aid. More important than the aid is how the person will access the aid. By this I mean how will they point to the options on the page, keyboard or screen to indicate what they want to say? Some people are able to point easily, or at least adequately, using a finger. Others may have difficulty with movement that makes isolating a finger to point difficult. Some might be able to use a fist to point and this will have implications for the size and arrangement of the options on the page. Some people might find it easier to use a no tech YES and NO response while a communication partner uses assisted scanning with them. Others may be able to use switches, joysticks or other adapted mouse options, eye pointing, head pointing or eye gaze technology.

## Direct access

The direct access option means that you point directly to the thing you want to activate or indicate. You might point with index finger, your fist, a mouse, a mouse alternative, your eyes or a pointer that you hold or wear on a headband. The key issue is that you point straight at the target. Direct access can be made easier by placing a key guard over the options. This is a template that covers the options producing a raised edge around each one. The person using it can use the raised edge to slip into the correct selection if they point slightly wide of their target.

## Supported access

The supported access option involves the communication partner being an integral part of the AAC user's ability to communicate. It might be as simple as assisted scanning or it might involve a programme of physical support such as facilitated communication training (FCT) or motor planning training (MPT). Both of these methods entail the provision of physical support so that a person who is trying to point to a communication aid is steadied so that they can make an accurate selection to their indented target. Supported access can be relevant for people using direct access or indirect access.

## Indirect access

The indirect access option is for people who have movement issues or visual issues that make direct access difficult and usually involves the use of switches. These act rather like the buttons you see on game shows that the players press to tell the host they have the answer. They can be used in a number of different ways including the following.

### TWO SWITCH SCANNING

Two switch scanning can be used with some light tech and most high tech aids. The person presses one switch to scan through the options available and a second switch to choose the one they want.

### ONE SWITCH AUTOMATIC SCAN

The one switch automatic scan is used with some light tech and most high tech aids. There is an automatic scan through the options (usually a light or a border round the option being scanned). The person stops the scan on the choice by pressing the switch.

### ONE SWITCH INVERSE OR RELEASE SCAN

The one switch inverse or release scan is used with some light tech and most high tech aids. It is similar to automatic scan except the person holds the switch down until they reach their choice when they let go.

### ONE SWITCH STEP SCAN

The one switch step scan is used with some light tech and most high tech aids. This involves pressing the switch in one way to set it off and in another way to select. It might be holding it down harder or for a longer period of time.

### AUDITORY PROMPT

Auditory prompt can be used with low tech, light tech and high tech aids. The auditory prompt involves a person, or the device itself, telling the person using it the options by speaking them out loud as they are scanned. This is very useful for people who have visual impairment or reasons why they cannot have their device in their visual field, for example, if they are carrying it in a back pack.

ASSISTED SCANNING

Assisted scanning can be used with low tech, light tech and high tech aids. In assisted scanning the communication partner either activates the scanning switch or just indicates each choice in turn until the person gives a YES response to let them know they have chosen. This is very useful for helping the person to develop their physical control. The communication partner can be more sensitive to their timing needs so that they experience more success than they might have done with an unforgiving automatically timed switch. They can help the person to become more successful by practising shortening times, etc.

## Investigating communication aids

There are a number of communication aid centres where children can be taken to test out, and sometimes borrow for trial purposes, various communication aids (see the Useful Addresses and Contacts section).

If children are at all delayed in speech acquisition and/or hand function it is a good idea to investigate switch-operated toys and communication strategies from as early an age as possible. Even if a child is going to acquire speech later on such devices give them an early access to two-way communication and some control over their environment.

Some of the machines can vary the amount of output between one phrase or word (using the whole screen as a switch) and anything up to 30 or more using sections on a screen. Children who have difficulty pressing a particular small section on a screen (perhaps because of difficulty with fine hand control movements) may be able to learn to scan and select from a large set of options using only one switch. There is a switch for everyone, whatever their difficulty with control over movement. Some operate on the lightest movement; some can be activated only by a muscle twitch or the interruption of a beam of light or even by only thinking. The Lightwriter is a device that speaks as the user types. It can also have a number of pre-recorded messages put on it for quick conversation.

## COMMUNICATION FOR CHILDREN WITH VISUAL IMPAIRMENT

If a child has restricted mobility and visual impairment, the carers and the speech and language therapists are set a challenging task to enable communication. It is very important to bring other senses (hearing, touch, taste and smell) into play with communication. The first level of communication is to enable a child to make choices and this could be done through many media. Examples include the following:

- Touching certain fabrics or other touch sensitive items which the child can relate to a desired object or activity. By touching the appropriate item the child can indicate choice.

- Making the visual clue very distinct and clear. This can be achieved either by using very contrasting colours or by using different fluorescent or reflective colours and/or shapes.

- Combining the hearing with touch. When the child hears a certain auditory clue she can press the appropriate indicator for her choice.

## COMMUNICATION FOR CHILDREN WITH HEARING IMPAIRMENT

As with visual impairment, the other senses (i.e. vision, touch, taste and smell) will assume greater importance to provide compensation. If the child has enough fine motor control of her hands, she should be enabled to start learning sign language at as early an age as possible. Even if she is unable to sign you can help to make your communications clear by signing to her and being generally physically expressive.

Sound can actually be felt through vibration even by someone who is completely deaf. Make sure she gets every opportunity to 'feel' as well as see things, especially items which have a sound element to them. Ensure she gets the opportunity to maximize learning through vision. Lots of books and other visual learning aids will help.

If the hearing deficit is sensory neural (i.e. part of the brain damage) it may be possible to stimulate improvement in hearing by presenting the stimuli of sound.

## COMMUNICATION FOR CHILDREN WITH DUAL SENSORY IMPAIRMENT

Dual sensory impairment is generally taken to mean impairment in both hearing and vision. In this case the sense of touch plays a vital role in communication. In the UK the organization SENSE has been set up to support people who have dual sensory impairment and can offer advice on special teaching techniques to facilitate communication: see www.sense. org.uk. See also the Useful Addresses and Contacts section. For similar organizations in the USA visit: www.deafblind.com/usa.html and in Australia: www.deafblind.com/australia.html

Supporting children to develop communication skills is crucial if they are to benefit from opportunities for community involvement.


## APPROACHES THAT REQUIRE PHYSICAL SUPPORT

It is natural to offer physical assistance to someone who is struggling with movement. Over the years therapists, educators and carers have provided physical support on a regular basis. Any physical task is easier to learn when you have a model from which to learn.


### Facilitated communication training

It is unfortunate that the use of FCT has been seen by some as a controversial technique. I would argue that this has happened because researchers have not always been asking the most useful research questions. Much of the research which has discredited FCT was testing the validity of messages communicated by people who have typed a message while receiving physical support. Very little research has asked questions about the impact of the technique on physical skill development or other aspects of development.

Like all techniques FCT, or FC as it is sometimes referred to, can be badly done. Because physical support is used, many researchers have responded by scrutinizing the physical support and testing for facilitator influence rather than examining what other factors might be contributing to the apparent increase in cognitive ability that often accompanies an FCT programme. There are an increasing number of people who can now point independently and who claim that FCT played a major part in their skill development. Improved pointing ability has meant that many of this group are able to type to communicate and can articulate the ways in which FCT helped them.

Lucy Black (2001) gives a powerful account of how her understanding of language improved as a result of her stumbling around the keyboard trying to make sense of it. Rosemary Crossley's (1994) guide remains the most comprehensive guide to FCT. Rosemary also wrote *Speechless* which is a book of case studies that are a testimony to the power of communication that can be developed through AAC (Crossley 2000).


### Motor planning training

Communication and Learning Enterprises (accessed 1 January 2010) has introduced an approach called MPT, which is an adaptation of FCT.

The aim of MPT technique is to use physical support to help a person who has communication and movement difficulties to improve their motor control so that they can point more accurately (Communication and Learning Enterprises (accessed 1 January 2010)). The use of prompt hierarchies are common practice in the special education system. There are two types of prompt hierarchy: decreasing prompt hierarchy and increasing prompt hierarchy.

DECREASING PROMPT HIERARCHY

Decreasing prompt hierarchy involves physical and verbal support using a 'most-to-least' approach. This means that the highest level of support is offered first, which is usually hand over hand guidance known as full physical assist (FPA). Next comes partial physical assist (PPA), which involves the provision of physical support at a minimal level, for example by touching the wrist to stabilize handwriting. Modelling involves showing the student what you want him to do. Gesture is pointing or using facial expression or otherwise indicating with some motion what you want the student to do. Direct verbal (DV) is a statement of what you want the student to do. Indirect verbal (IV) tells the student that something is expected of him but not exactly what. Independence is when the student is able to carry out a task without any prompts or assistance.

INCREASING PROMPT HIERARCHY

Increasing prompt hierarchy involves offering prompts in the exact reverse of the decreasing prompt hierarchy. This is used when you want the student to attempt the task independently and then bring in increasingly more supportive prompts until you find the least level of support required for the student to succeed at the task. The idea is that the level of support required should decrease over successive attempts of similar tasks. See Homeschooling Kids With Disabilities at www.members.tripod.com/~Maaja/

STRUCTURE OF MPT

MPT has some resemblance to the second of these two prompt hierarchies but has a much more complex structure as follows:

- An assessment from an MPT assessor and trainer is required before someone can embark on the programme. This will involve finding the minimal level of physical support that will enable a person to begin to successfully point to a choice.

- There is a training programme that practitioners must complete before they can claim to be supporting an MPT programme.

- No claims are made regarding authorship of communication while physical support is being provided.

- Independent alternatives that can run alongside physically supported pointing are sought in an ongoing way.

- Record keeping is essential so that fading of support can be monitored and so that a portfolio of communication expressed while physical support was offered can be examined. Consistencies and sharing of novel information is highlighted giving validation to communication.

- Ongoing monitoring is provided by an experienced trainer.

Here are some UK websites which aim to keep up-to-date information available on AAC in general:

- The AAC Self-Assessment Tool-Kit: www.candleaac.com/ AACTool-Kit.htm

- About AAC: www.communicationmatters.org.uk/about-aac

- Ace Centre North Information Sheets: www.ace-north.org.uk/ pages/resources/infosheets.asp

Chapter 7

# DAY TO DAY LIFE

This chapter aims to give you useful tips for helping your child in her day to day life.

## MOBILITY

Mobility is more than getting from one place to another – it is movement. Many children who have cerebral palsy will have varying degrees of difficulty with movement. For some, walking may be the only problem. For others hand function will be impaired. In more severe cases there may be difficulties in all movement including the movement of the child's head from left to right and up and down, and the rotation of the trunk and pelvis.

There is more than one way to tackle difficulties with mobility. The two main approaches involve working to improve mobility with exercises and purposeful play on the one hand, and on the other, making changes to the environment so that limitations in mobility place less restriction on a child's enjoyment of life.

### Exercises

Your community or hospital physiotherapist may give you an exercise programme which you can carry out in your home. You may also receive training in ways of handling your child to inhibit unwanted movement. If they do not offer this, *ask for it*. The physiotherapist helps children to achieve much more by teaching their carers how to carry out simple exercises and proper handling on a regular basis. The physiotherapist should also explain the purpose of the exercises so that you know what your aims are and are able to monitor progress. Ask whether your physiotherapist is trained in Bobath. If not, ask your physiotherapist to find out more about Bobath. You can ask your consultant to refer you to the Bobath centre for assessment.

Some basic Bobath exercises can be carried out without interfering with your own life too dramatically. For example, while your child is very young you can give her a good stretch at the same time as sitting down watching television. You are likely to have your child on your lap to read stories to her. At the same time you can be holding her in such a way that her posture is being corrected.

In every activity it will be helpful to your child if her posture is taken into account and rectified, whether you are walking in the park, playing in the garden, playing in the house or just sitting down in front of the television together. It need not be a chore as, with practice, it becomes second nature to keep your child's positioning and movements stable. As she grows older your early training should reap rewards and she will become able to self-correct automatically. It is also essential that you teach anyone who is likely to handle your child for any length of time the correct way to hold her. Otherwise you are likely to become frustrated and feel that only you can be trusted with your child. This will only add to your stress.

The first priority for a child who has cerebral palsy is to avoid contractures (permanent tightening or slacking of the muscles) which could ultimately cause deformity (bone structure growing incorrectly). The likelihood of contractures increases with the severity of the mobility restriction. The second priority is to enable your child to move as nearly as possible in normal motor patterns. This will give her the greatest opportunity to feel comfortable and confident.

In the UK there are a number of publications which can be obtained through Scope which offer advice to parents on physiotherapy in the home. See the Useful Addresses and Contacts section for details of similar organizations in other countries.

## DIET AND NUTRITION

Children with CP are often using a surprising amount of energy even if they are not very mobile. Muscle spasm, for example, uses energy. A well-balanced diet is essential for all of us. Many children with CP are likely to have difficulties with eating certain foods because of chewing and/or swallowing problems. If you need practical help your consultant or GP may be able to refer you to a dietician who can advise on the kind of diet your child needs and a speech and language therapist can advise on the actual method of feeding.

Try to ensure that you separate out the different tastes as your child grows. If she has problems with developing the ability to chew, there are techniques you can use to help the development of chewing such as offering dried apricots or fruit straps in between meals. For children who would find these difficult you can still encourage the chewing reflex by allowing them to chew on (but not swallow) a piece of fruit securely wrapped in a piece of muslin which you can control so that they do not need to deal with the swallowing of solid food. If you are able, try to vary the texture of different foods given to your child. For example, I have found that I can give Dan the meat section of his meal with a grainier texture by putting it through a coffee grinder rather than puréeing it. All attempts at varying texture will add to a child's eating development and enjoyment of food.

Make sure that your child has a good balanced diet with proteins (found in meat, eggs, cheese and beans), carbohydrates (found in potatoes and bread), roughage (found in oats, wheat germ and green vegetables), fats (found in butter and oil), vitamins and minerals (found in fruit and vegetables), and plenty of fluids. You should be advised by a health visitor or dietician about the amount of calories your child should receive for his or her weight. If it is difficult to provide enough in the normal way, you could consider adding food supplements or fortified drinks to their diet. You can also mix normal foods in a way which increase protein, carbohydrate or fat content without adding too much bulk. For example, banana, honey, cream and/or egg can be added to a simple breakfast cereal to considerably enhance its calorie content.

## Feeding

Self-feeding can begin as early as nine months. Small babies automatically bring everything they handle to their mouths. Eventually this is turned into the skill to bring food to their mouths. With teaching from carers, children learn to turn an automatic reaction into a deliberate and quite sophisticated activity. Some children who have cerebral palsy will miss out on these early learning opportunities. They can be helped enormously if their parents are taught to compensate by helping them to feed themselves from the appropriate age.

To get advice on this one aspect of a child's daily life, you may have to go to as many as five different professionals. The physiotherapist concentrates on the best positioning of your child. The dietician can advise on the best kinds of food to give her. The speech and language therapist can advise on the best ways to achieve a good chewing pattern and mouth closure. The occupational therapist can advise on appropriate feeding equipment and seating. Finally, you may need to discuss any digestive problems with the consultant. In order to give relevant advice it is essential that these professionals observe your child while she is eating, and it is preferable for them to work together to ensure that they do not give contradictory advice. However, it is not an easy task to gather so many experts together at the right time for such a consultation and, even if you can, it is highly unlikely that a child will be willing to carry on her normal feeding routine with such an audience. At the end of the day it is up to the carer and child to work out the most suitable feeding routine, having taken as much advice from various sources as they can.

Make sure your child can see the plate, the food which is on it and the spoon bringing the food from the plate to her mouth. This is especially important for children with hearing impairment. Talk to her about the process and let her see, feel and smell the food, feel the plate and the spoon, and get a sense of their proximity to each other and to her.

Children without disabilities go through a stage when they get very messy during feeding. There is a danger that carers of children who have disabilities will keep their children extra clean either because it is easier to do so because they are not attempting to feed themselves or because the carer feels (maybe even subconsciously) that it accentuates the 'look' of disability.

It is important that you are aware of where the food is ending up. If food is left around a child's mouth throughout a meal, it may cause her to lose sensitivity or the 'feel' of where the food should be. However, there is no harm in a child with disabilities getting the same opportunity to experience food fully by getting her hands in it for example.

It is important to ensure that the child can see the spoon coming to her mouth when you are doing the feeding, and there are various techniques to encourage good chewing and mouth closure which a speech and language therapist may be able to advise on. Some children with CP have difficulty keeping their mouths closed and/or have a habit of thrusting out their tongue when trying to eat. It can also take a long time to move from the mouth movements associated with sucking from the breast or bottle to the rounded chew required to break down solid food in the mouth. If your child has difficulties with this, the move from sucking to chewing may need to be encouraged slowly and patiently by very gradually increasing the density of texture and later on the 'lumpiness' of the food offered. Some children with CP have difficulty with their gag reflex. This means that they find it hard to cough up bits of food that go down the wrong way. If this is a particular problem for your child, advice should be sought from a speech and language therapist or your paediatric consultant.

While your child needs your assistance with eating, you could give her the opportunity to attempt some self-help with feeding at each meal, provided you are satisfied that she has eaten sufficient food for nourishment. This can be done however severely affected a child is. At the very least you can place a spoon in the child's hand and guide it as far as is comfortable to give her first-hand experience. If she is able to get her hand to her mouth you can guide the spoon all the way. You can also encourage her to pick up food (such as cakes, biscuits, bread or fruit) in her hands and bring it to her own mouth. Make sure, however, that such an activity does not contribute to her receiving insufficient nutrition. If in doubt consult a dietician to ensure that your child is getting an adequate diet before introducing this kind of self-help.

## Breast feeding or bottle feeding the young baby

These days mothers are encouraged to breast feed whenever possible, especially for the first few weeks of a child's life. It has now been established that the very early breast milk contains many different factors which help the baby to build up her natural immune system. Children who have been in special care, tube fed or even just slow to feed at the breast may have difficulty getting enough breast milk to sustain them. It is possible to feed the early breast milk to the baby via the tube feeding method and milk can be expressed into bottles so that the baby can still benefit from mother's natural milk even if she cannot suck at the breast. It may be possible to supplement breast feeding with commercial preparations. Care should be taken that you do not deplete your supply of breast milk if you are supplementing. The breast needs to be stimulated by regular sucking to enable the production of more milk. There are breast feeding counsellors in many places.

## DENTAL CARE

Children who have CP may be more susceptible to tooth decay than their non-disabled peers. This is because the natural self-cleaning which is facilitated by saliva (especially at night) may be disrupted. In addition, debris which usually gets moved away by the motion of the tongue may not be cleared so effectively if a child's tongue is less mobile.

Regular brushing of teeth is vital. You should start to clean your baby's teeth as soon as they appear in the mouth. When brushing your child's teeth try to develop a technique which is consistent. Work around your child's mouth brushing two or three teeth at a time in a circular or 'mini scrub' motion. Pay particular attention to the inner surfaces and the small, difficult to clean spaces between teeth, and the biting surfaces of the teeth at the back of the mouth. Using a battery operated toothbrush might help to make teeth cleaning easier.

Dental treatment can be very distressing for a young child. It is better to prevent the need if at all possible. In some areas there are specialist dentists who are trained in special needs. Ask your consultant, your GP or your regular dentist for advice on this.

## THE IMPORTANCE OF HAND FUNCTION

Many children with CP will have no problems with mobility in the upper part of their bodies. However, a significant number do. It is important that children get every opportunity to experience the world with their hands. During my own research I found that whether their child would walk was the second most common concern for most carers. Very few respondents noted the importance of hand function. Many professionals and adults with disabilities would contend that hand function is far more necessary for independence than walking. You can get around in a wheelchair if the right facilities (such as ramps and lifts) are available in the environment but it is more difficult to produce mechanical aids which can take over the fine motor role played by the hands.

Encourage your child to use his hands as actively as he can from as young an age as possible. While he is still a baby, make sure he has mobiles and dangling toys to reach out to. If your child has a visual or hearing impairment choose mobiles while also make a sound, arc very brightly coloured and, if possible, have different textures.

As the child gets older ensure that he is offered interesting and varied opportunities to use his hands in play. Encourage him to use his hands to play with toys appropriate to his age (with help if necessary) – for example, knocking down and building with bricks, and play dough. Later still you can encourage him to push, pull and pick up his toys. If your child has very restricted hand movement it might still be possible for him to use his hands to press a touch sensitive switch. A speech or language therapist may be able to assist or you may be able to seek advice from a communication aids centre.

## PLAY

Play is an essential activity for all children. This is where real learning begins. It may not be easy for some children who have CP to engage in spontaneous play so you will need to be ready to give whatever assistance you can to help them enjoy playing. This is an area where you can fully involve friends and family in supporting you in helping your child to develop.

Because CP is such a varied condition ranging from very mild disability to total immobility, it is difficult to prescribe exactly how to be enabling in a general guide like this one. You will need to ensure that your child's toys are readily available, easy to get at and that she has some way of letting you know what she wants to play with at any given time. As she gets older, and depending on the degree of her disability, she will be able to indicate this in a clear and certain way. However, you need to ensure that she doesn't miss out on the early opportunity to make choices in the area of play. As early as possible you need to establish a way for her to indicate preferences. This may be through speech or signs and, later on, through sign boards or electronic communications. If your child is slow to develop speech, a speech and language therapist can help you and your child to find the quickest and easiest method of communication.

The following play ideas are graded from the very young upwards. I'm sure there are lots more ideas that you can think up for yourself. A mirror can be a great aid in playing so that your child can get visual feedback on what she is doing. It can even be actively introduced into play by enabling the child to, for example, smear shaving cream on to a mirror or blow bubbles towards one.

## Play ideas for 0–3 years

- Play mat and frame with dangling toys.

- Rattles and windmills.

- Rocking and bouncing games.

- Making lots of babbling and cooing noises.

- Tickling games.

- Building bricks – begin with building them up for her to knock down, later on help her to build her own towers to knock down.

- Picture books – you can also get picture books which have the complement of sounds and raised textures to stimulate hearing and touch.

- Hide and seek with toys and people behind curtains, under towels, etc.

- Hitting things – wooden spoons on saucepans for example.

- Imitation and turn taking.

- Playing with mirrors.

- Unwrapping toys (don't put tape on wrapping paper).

- Water and sand.

- Lentils, rice and pasta in tubs to sit in, put your hands in or just throw about.

You need to be careful to watch that children don't put small objects in their mouths that they might choke on.

## Play ideas for 1–3 years

- Posting box games.

- Finger puppets.

- Tunnel games.

- Surprise bags full of toys and interesting objects for your child to find.

- Pulling and pushing.

- Lucky dip.

- Picking correct object from a selection, for example, you can ask your child to find you the cow from a selection of farmyard animals.

- Pretend games with dollies and teddies.

- Painting, using fingers or brushes.

- Cars and trains.

## Play ideas for 2–4 years

- Story books.

- Helping round the house.

- Making cakes and other food.

- Ball games.

- Obstacle courses.

- Messy play with a purpose (i.e. sculptures in sand, boats on water).

- Play dough modelling.

- Sticking textures on paper with non-toxic glue.

- Printing (potato prints, etc.).

- Spot the difference.

- Shape and colour matching.

- Make believe.

- 'Simon says' type copying games.

- Toy shops.

- Turning cardboard boxes into toys (such as castles, cars or space ships).

- Lego/Duplo.

- Action rhymes.

- Listening games.

- Making music with homemade instruments.

## SEATING

Some children who have CP can manage well enough with an ordinary chair. If this is not the case, is your child using a chair which holds her firmly in position but at the same time allows her some freedom of movement in her hands, arms and upper trunk? Good seating is essential for all of us and particularly so for a child who has CP as they may need to be seated more than the average child and many activities will be likely to take place in a sitting position. There are numerous alternatives. Standard special seating is available through occupational therapists but these chairs can sometimes be designed to hold a child firmly in place rather than to allow freedom of movement and therefore only tackle half the needs. You could experiment with ordinary high chairs supplemented with the creative use of cushions and foam padding if needed. For this you will need your local children's store to be willing to let you spend some time experimenting on their premises to ensure that you don't waste your money buying inappropriate furniture. There are seating clinics to which you can be referred which are particularly useful if your child is likely to spend a lot of time sitting down. See the Useful Addresses and Contacts section for addresses of centres which specialize in appliances and equipment, including seating.

## APPLIANCES AND EQUIPMENT

Everyday life poses enormous problems for people who have restricted mobility and movements they cannot control. There is an enormous range of specialized equipment designed to help compensate for this from the earliest age into adulthood. However, the first problem is finding out what choices exist. The second problem is finding the substantial finance that such equipment often requires. The other major problem is that standardized equipment cannot easily be tailored to suit the needs of every individual. Occupational therapists are the professionals who are trained in the use of equipment but they may not have the most up-to-date information on what is available.

There are a number of walking frames available both from the statutory and private sector. State provided wheelchairs may be of a standard type. Sophisticated chairs may not be available unless you can fund them yourself or unless you can provide evidence that your child is a special case. Funding may also be available for special beds (e.g. you may need to get a bed which you can lower and raise to facilitate dressing as well as getting in and out of bed). Examples of adaptations to the home for which you might be able to get funding including moving bedrooms and bathrooms to ground floor level, lowering the sink and cooker in the kitchen, and lowering light switches.

For all equipment, appliances and adaptations, state funding will depend on assessment and recommendation from the appropriate professional. To be sure you have examined all of the alternatives it is worth contacting organizations, such as the Disabled Living Foundation, which specializes in equipment in the UK (see the Useful Addresses and Contacts section which includes details for USA). Funding for equipment is not always easy to obtain. There are a number of charities who will consider making one-off grants to provide equipment which you are unable to get through the state system. Your local library should have a list of grant-making trusts.

Equipment designed specifically for conductive education is economical, attractive, versatile and comprehensive. While conductive education equipment may not be appropriate for every child it can offer the opportunity for children to maximize their independence and is extremely space saving.

## FLOOR PLAY

One of the most valuable pieces of advice I ever received regarding Dan's needs was to 'put him on the floor'. A child's earliest independence comes from exploring the world, using whatever mobility he has, from a position where he is free to do so. Putting a child on the floor, even if he has very little mobility, at least allows for the possibility of exploration. Time spent lying on the floor with a few toys around will be a valuable opportunity to exercise early self-help in play and mobility.

Because our children have special needs we can easily get caught in a trap of thinking that we must always be controlling our children's positioning and activities but *all* children must have the chance to learn from experience. If you are offering a lot of stimulation to your child (input), there has to be an opportunity for him to show you what he has learned (output) by being allowed a free rein occasionally. Putting him on the floor to explore is one way to enable this.

## STIMULATING CHILDREN WITH SENSORY IMPAIRMENT

Sensory impairment does not apply to all children who have CP, but many do have disabilities additional to motor disorder. Any of the five senses can be involved in sensory impairment. Severely affected children may begin life with all five senses impaired. It has been found that appropriate stimulation at an early stage can help the child to defeat, or at least to lessen, sensory impairment.

### Vision

Cortical visual impairment is sometimes a problem which accompanies CP. It means that the child does not seem to see, or does not seem to see well (due to damage in the visual cortex of the brain), even though the eyes appear to function properly. This is a condition which may persist into adulthood but, in many cases, may recover to some extent. Stimulation of the eyes by using lights and bright colours can be of enormous benefit in helping the recovery process. Ensure that the room is always brightly lit when the child is doing any activity unless you are deliberately wishing to isolate bright objects such as coloured bulbs, etc. The following tips may help you to create some enjoyable visual stimulation for your child:

- You could make a play mat out of shiny paper covered with sticky-backed clear plastic (the kind you can buy in rolls for covering textbooks, etc.) You can further add to the effect by scattering glitter and other shiny objects under the plastic. You can add squeaky buttons to bring auditory stimulation and pleasure into the game.

- Set up Christmas lights and Christmas decorations on a frame for your child to play under.

- Get an ultraviolet light and rig it up in a room where you can cut out other lights. Show your child shapes cut out of fluorescent paper under the ultraviolet light. There has been some concern that too much exposure to ultra-violent can be harmful (such as causing cataracts) so be very careful not to keep your child under the light for very long.

- Get hold of some disco lights and let her enjoy frequent light shows.

- Make sure you have a bright light shining on her toys when you are playing with her.

- In Dan's early days he had a lot of success with one of those space blankets used by runners after marathons. They are very shiny, make a noise at the slightest touch and move easily with only a very small amount of manipulation.

## Hearing

If your child has sensory neural impairment which has some potential for recovery, sound may still play a central role in activities. Ensure that a visual or tactile clue accompanies all sounds which are presented to stimulate hearing. Toys which vibrate as well as sound are helpful. If you place your hands on a speaker you will feel the reverberation of the sound. If you play a drum, the vibration can be felt as well as heard. Disco lights which flash in time to the music can help your child to develop a sense of rhythm.

It may help to judge as well as stimulate a child's hearing if you gradually reduce the volume of a piece of music in a play session. Be expressive when you communicate. Use sign language as well as speech even if your child is not learning to communicate with signing.

## Sensitivity (or lack of) to touch

Some children with CP will start life very sensitive to touch or seemingly lacking the full sense of touch. Hugging and kissing is a nurturing and effective way to begin the process of desensitization. Some children will not like to be touched at first but, if you persevere, they are likely to overcome this.

Toys and books which explore different textures are readily available from shops such as early learning centres and may be helpful for children who have visual impairment as well as those who need tactile stimulation.

## Taste and smell

Food and drink are obvious media for stimulation of taste and smell. Make sure you offer a varied and interesting selection. I have also found pot-pourri very useful. As well as having an interesting smell, children can get their hands in it for tactile stimulation. Aromatherapy oils such as lavender, camomile, mandarin (from about six months old), sandalwood, tea-tree and eucalyptus (very good for colds), orange, grapefruit, lemon, rose (for those who can afford it!), myrtle, geranium and ylang-ylang offer pleasing olfactory stimulation as well as having therapeutic benefits.

To stimulate taste buds you can offer your child a variety of small tastes of warm and cold things and sharp, sour, sweet, etc. Examples are ice lollies, pieces of lemon, honey, tiny tastes of yeast extract, yoghurt, etc.

# INVOLVING YOUR CHILD IN FAMILY LIFE

Involve your child fully in family life. Let him help with chores if he is able. If he is not able, explain to him what you are doing. All children love making cakes. Even if mobility is severely affected he can still enjoy this activity with help. Children love to follow their parents around while they are doing the housework or the garden. If he can't do this, make sure he knows what you are doing and take some time to help him copy you. Children usually love watching television. I would recommend that a child who has CP should get the opportunity of the stimulation television can offer at least on a controlled basis, especially where the carer's time is severely restricted. It is better than leaving a child without any stimulation. A trip to the shops is interesting for a child even if it is a pain for the parent. There is a lot to be learned on the shelves in the supermarket.

If a child with disabilities is to have every opportunity to grow up with perceptions of the world which are similar to his non-disabled peers, full involvement with everyday activities is essential. Too much segregation and 'specialized' activity increase disadvantage by setting him further apart. Many so-called success stories of adults with CP occur where as children they lived in busy, active families in which they were treated as near to the same as everyone else as their disability allowed.

# Chapter 8

# COMPLEMENTARY THERAPY

There has been a general shift in attitude over recent years in regard to the use of complementary therapy. What used to be considered 'cranky' and 'off beat' is often now recognized to have a basis in fact. Many of the so-called alternative treatments available nowadays have direct parallels in the more conventional medical system.

Treatments which have been used for centuries have been adopted by science but brought under a more controlled environment which can be clinically tested. Herbalism is a good example of this trend. Many pharmaceutical drugs administered by doctors are chemical compounds which have been synthesized from the exact same ingredients found in the herbal remedy which can be used in its place.

Complementary medicine is no more able to cure cerebral palsy than conventional methods. However, there may be more gentle, enjoyable and even more effective ways to alleviate some of the effects of cerebral palsy. Complementary therapy is often used in a curative or preventative way for common illnesses which can cause more distress to a child who has CP. There is disagreement within the conventional medical community as to the effectiveness of certain complementary treatments.

The therapies outlined in this chapter are not an exhaustive list but they are the most commonly available forms of alternative treatment. Names and addresses of therapy centres and organizations which specialize in the various techniques can be found in the Useful Addresses and Contacts section.

Many complementary methods take a different view of the diagnosis of a condition from that of mainstream western medicine. Conventional medicine observes symptoms (problems which are presented and are directly observable) and seeks to alleviate the distress caused by symptoms or to eliminate the symptoms by suppressing them, usually with the use of drugs and/or surgery.

Complementary systems prefer to observe the 'whole person'. Symptoms are seen in the context of a person's overall physical and emotional health. They also attempt to examine and treat causes rather than symptoms. To do this alternative practitioners will take detailed histories of their patients and will seek to identify the central weakness which may be causing a chain reaction of ill health and which may well present as illness in another part of the body altogether.

It is essential with all forms of treatment, and complementary medicine is no exception, that you consult a practitioner in the field rather than administering for yourself out of layperson's guides. Few of the following methods have been researched under the conventional 'double blind' clinical trials model but many people who use complementary medicine have observed their positive effects. In China research concentrates on the relative effectiveness of different combinations for a given condition. The negative side-effects of trying out complementary methods are far fewer than those often experienced under conventional medical treatment. Having said this it would be irresponsible to stop taking conventional medicine that has been prescribed by a doctor. Sometimes a complementary alternative can be used alongside conventional medicine. You can then discuss the possibility of reducing conventional medicine but this must be done under the guidance of a medical practitioner.

## ACUPUNCTURE

Acupuncture has been used as a conventional medicine in China for as long as records exist and is still a major treatment system often alongside western techniques which have found their way into Chinese medicine. It can also be provided on the National Health Service in the UK for certain conditions such as back pain. Diagnosis is carried out by measuring the energy flow in a number of meridians which form pathways (similar to a very fine nervous system) throughout the body. The energy levels are measured by taking pulses (of which the system identifies 27). The ten internal organs (gallbladder, liver, lungs, colon, stomach, spleen, heart, small intestine, bladder and kidney) are perceived to carry the burden of any imbalance in the body. The vocabulary of acupuncture is very different from that of conventional medicine. The basic elements of water, wood, fire, earth and metal are considered to be reflected in the human body and an imbalance in these elements may be perceived as causal. There is also an emphasis on achieving a balance, in the body, of the opposite (but not antagonistic) qualities of yin and yang. Yin is cold, dark and feminine and yang is warm, light and masculine. A balance of both of these qualities is considered necessary for health. The energy flow which passes down the meridians is known as ch'i (pronounced 'chee'). Skin colour and body odour will also be noted and taken into account in diagnosis as well as a patient's fears, dislikes and preferences; for example, for seasons, drinks and colours. The organs are considered to have a mother and child relationship and stimulation given to the mother organ will be expected to treat the child organ. For example, the kidney/bladder is mother to the liver/ gallbladder and stimulation to the meridian of the kidney will automatically stimulate the liver.

Treatment is carried out by stimulating various points on the meridian which enable ch'i to flow more freely and affect the organ identified as causing problems. Stimulation will be in the form of acupuncture (using a fine needle which is partially inserted into the skin), acupressure (using fingertip pressure) or moxa (the application of heat). Many acupuncturists supplement their treatment with Chinese herbs to be taken in between treatment sessions. Many of the painful or distressing symptoms which occur as a result of having cerebral palsy may be lessened by acupuncture. Also, diagnosis by an acupuncturist may reveal conditions which have gone unnoticed by traditional methods. Examples of treatable conditions may be: constipation, colic, high muscle tone (tight muscles), spasms, convulsions, depression, lethargy, poor concentration and sleeplessness.

It is possible that acupuncturists may reveal an unexpected underlying cause for symptoms you present to them. I took Dan to an acupuncturist with a view to getting treatment for his spasms and tightness of muscle. After taking a detailed history and examining Dan, he informed me that Dan had had colic all of his life and that was probably contributing not only to frequency of spasm and tightness of muscle but also to poor appetite, constipation and difficulty sleeping. He also said that Dan was extremely cold and gave him moxa treatment to counter this. After one treatment Dan's stomach was more relaxed than it had ever been before and his general tightness relaxed a little. I had always assumed that his tight muscles were purely the result of brain damage but, in fact, his upset digestive system was significantly contributing to the problem and this is treatable. His spasms increased initially but then settled down to a lesser level than prior to treatment. Dan also benefits from traditional western medicine to reduce acid.

## Shiatsu massage

Shiatsu involves the correction of faulty circulation, improvement of metabolism and treatment of a number of ailments by massage to meridia connecting points just beneath the surface of the skin. The technique is based on Japanese acupuncture theory and uses the same points but applies pressure and massage rather than using needles.

## HOMOEOPATHY

Homoeopathy is based on the principle that 'like cures like'. A minute dose of a preparation is administered which emulates the condition being treated in order to combat that condition. Homoeopaths believe in the body's ability to heal itself, and see symptoms as the body's way of striving to achieve that cure. The symptoms must therefore reach an extreme peak in order for the body to effectively carry out its self-healing function. The role of the homoeopath is to find the homoeopathic drug which will enable to body to carry out this function. The current use of vaccinations under conventional medicine uses a similar principle to that of homoeopathy but without the detailed analysis which this school of medicine engages in.

During treatment symptoms are expected to worsen in the initial phase. Homoeopaths believe that symptoms are indications of the body's healing process and that the clue to treatment lies with the person. They will attempt to understand the person in terms of personality, current stresses in life, state of mind and preferences and dislikes in order to support the patient in battling against whatever condition is causing him discomfort. Since the 1830s in excess of 2000 substances which produce certain symptoms have been developed by homoeopaths. As with Chinese medicine the effects of weather, time of day, seasons, atmosphere and many other outside influences on the patient's symptoms will be considered. The quality of bodily excretion will be taken into account.

Many of the substances used in homoeopathy are poisonous if given in sufficient quantity but the quantity is the key to this form of treatment. Extremely diluted doses are often found to be the most effective. Homoeopathic remedies tend to be highly diluted for chronic conditions and diluted to a lower degree for acute conditions.

The homoeopath is committed to discovering the deepest and most individual remedy for each person, taking on board that person's unique symptoms and reactions to the environment as well as their moods and likes and dislikes.

Treatment is given in the form of small pills, which sometimes are dissolvable. They taste of sugar and contain minute doses of the chosen homoeopathic remedy which has been diluted to the required level for the type of condition and the person being treated. Once administered, and if the remedy is working at its most effective, the symptoms being treated will probably intensify or get worse before they gradually disappear. Your homoeopath will be able to advise you regarding the length of time this process is likely to take. Some homoeopathic remedies are available in the form of ointment for treating skin conditions, stings and bruising, etc. Some remedies are designed to offer instant relief in cases such as injury, shock and some other acute conditions.

## HERBALISM

The use of herbs to treat illness has been available in most cultures throughout history. Herbs fell from favour as conventional medicine began to take hold during the 18th century. However, the use of herbs has remained fairly commonplace even though their medicinal properties are no longer recognized by the medical profession. I remember when I was working in a nursing home for elderly people being surprised to find that the elderly ladies knew all about the healing properties of comfrey which I had recently discovered. Comfrey is a traditional soother for rubbed skin and bruising. Occasionally, medical scientific investigations will identify the healing properties of a herbal preparation (as has happened with a Chinese herbal remedy for skin conditions). When this happens the research tends to focus on developing a chemical compound which will synthetically reproduce the same effect and which can then be mass produced by pharmaceutical companies. Chemical compounds are preferred by the medical profession because they are easier to control, monitor and administer than their natural equivalents. Herbalists maintain that chemical compounds tend to have more severe side-effects than the natural herb. Natural herbs are more suitable in their immediate effect on the body and tend to diffuse more easily into the system which is therefore more able to accommodate the preparation. Chemical alternatives are often more severe and limited to the specific symptoms which a condition presents.

Herbalism, in a similar way to homoeopathy, aims to restore lost balance in the body by supporting the body's own 'self-righting' mechanisms. By administering the whole plant, rather than a specific derivative from a plant, a more wide-ranging effect is achieved providing a general enhancing of resistance or of the functioning of a particular system in the body. Herbalists do not reject conventional medicine. Rather, they are likely to maintain that early treatment with gentle plant remedies when the first signs of poor health occur can often restore a healthy balance without the need for recourse to more drastic drug treatment. For example, antibiotics, used sparingly in serious situations (such as pneumonia), can be valuable and life-saving. However, if suitable plant remedies had been prescribed as soon as early symptoms of infection (raised temperature, catarrh, etc.) were evident, the infection may possibly have been arrested and resolved at a much earlier stage. This is a useful website for general information about herbal supplements: www.herbal-supplement-resource.com/

The remedies suggested below are suitable for everyone and may specifically be useful in common health problems affecting children who have cerebral palsy. These herbs are all gentle in action and readily available. Most can be given as teas. The dose is not critical but two teaspoons of dried herb per cup is a standard rough guide for adults. This should be halved for children and halved again for small babies. Teas are made by adding boiling water to the herb and allowing it to stand (covered so that volatile oils are not lost in evaporation) for 5–10 minutes. Then strain and sweeten, if desired, with apple concentrate or honey. Give three or four times daily.

## Respiratory infections

Colds, coughs, catarrh and sore throat can be treated with the following:

- *Sage* is particularly good as a gargle or drunk slowly for sore throats. Sage can also be used as an infusion wrapped in muslin in the bath to aid muscles to relax.

- *Thyme* is too strong for very young children but useful added to sage for sore throats and minor chest infections.

- *Elderflower* is excellent for upper respiratory catarrh, induces sweating and sleep.

- *Yarrow* is another good remedy for stimulating elimination by sweating.

- *Hyssop* is useful for chest infections and chronic catarrh (an expectorant).

- *Elecampane* is very good for chest infections and for use as an expectorant. The root is used so a decoction has to be made – add cold water to the shredded root and allow to stand overnight before bringing to the boil.

- *Garlic* is marvellous for preventing and curing infection. Chop up the cloves finely and add them to honey so that the mixture may be swallowed without chewing. One or two teaspoons of the mixture should be given at bedtime. Fresh lemon juice may be added to the mixture. Garlic is powerfully bactericidal and is excreted via the lungs (hence the smell on the breath) so is particularly appropriate for chest infections. It sounds dreadful but actually doesn't taste that bad. Many children will take this mixture without protest.

## Sleeplessness and nervous excitability

Gentle calming herbs include *chamomile, lemon balm* and *lime flowers*. It is also worth trying these gentle herbs if your child is having lots of fits. There are other herbs traditionally used for treating fits but a qualified herbalist should be consulted before these are considered.

## Constipation

This useful website includes many potential solutions for constipation: www. umm.edu/altmed/articles/constipation-000041.htm

## OSTEOPATHY AND CRANIAL OSTEOPATHY

In common with other alternative practitioners, osteopaths believe that their treatment should seek to enable the body's own healing mechanisms to correct any imbalance which has developed and which is causing pain, discomfort or illness.

Osteopathy is particularly appropriate for treating conditions which arise as a result of muscular or skeletal dysfunction. Dysfunction is seen to arise and to worsen as a result of the brain's response to muscular or skeletal tension or alignment. The brain is constantly monitoring every muscle and joint and is accustomed to a set of norms for muscular tension and the position of joints. If a joint (e.g. a vertebra) jolts out of alignment due to an accident or for any other reason, a flood of impulses report the injury to the brain. Muscles which support the spine will tense up to protect the area and the brain reassesses 'normal' and tries to accommodate the body's new state. As a result, after the injury has healed the tension in the surrounding muscles may remain thereby rendering the joint susceptible to further injury or permanently out of line and unable to return to the normal, relaxed state.

Osteopathy works at ways to allow the body to reset its own norms which are then translated to the brain so that the original state of equilibrium is restored. At its most extreme this is achieved by the osteopath delivering small movements with high force on to the special problem area/joint with the intention of sending a more appropriate set of impulses through the muscular system and message to the brain.

Cranial osteopathy is more complex than conventional osteopathy. It works on the principle that the body contains a number of basic rhythms (e.g. breathing circulation, primary respiratory movement in all of the body's tissues and cranial sacrum rhythm). The whole body flexes and extends slightly in its natural state and these movements are reflected in the movement of the cranium. The cranium is the bone structure which surrounds the brain and which interlocks but also has flexibility which enables flexion and extension to take place within the skull area up to 6–10 times per minute. These movements can react upon movement in the brain, spinal cord, sacrum and limbs. Underlying cranial osteopathy is the notion that we develop patterns during our lives which may cause restriction in the natural flow of flexion and extension. Cranial osteopaths set out to correct any imbalance by enabling the cranial area to recover its natural flow.

Osteopathy cannot cure the brain damage which causes cerebral palsy. It is possible, however, that a number of the incorrect patterns of muscular tension and skeletal position which result from the brain damage send back further incorrect messages to the brain which further exacerbate the negative effects of the muscular and skeletal system. It is possible that osteopathy, gently and sensitively applied, may be able to avert a chain reaction which often creates more extreme tension and bone deformity than the original brain damage warrants.

## REFLEXOLOGY

The main principle of reflexology is that there is a direct reflex action between the nerve endings in the feet and various organs in the body. Light pressure applied to the appropriate nerve ending in the foot which correlates to an affected organ is said to bring relief to the condition caused by that particular organ dysfunction. This system can be used to diagnose, prevent and treat disorders. The reflexologist holds the patient's feet and uses sensitive fingers to read the surface. During treatment a stable pressure is maintained on the appropriate point of the foot while a clockwise rotating movement of the hand is applied continuously.

Reflexology is one of the few alternative techniques to have been researched with patients who have CP (Rong-zhi 1996, p.26). Many patients have reported that pain and spasm decreased. Reflexology is thought to be particularly useful in the treatment of congestion, constipation, dispersal of toxins in the body and improvement of energy flow.

## AROMATHERAPY

Aromatherapy is an ancient healing technique based on the use of aromatic essential oils and essences extracted from flowers, plants, resins and other substances. The treatment is absorbed through the skin (the body's largest organ) and passes very quickly into the bloodstream. Treatment is applied through gentle massage. The physical benefits of massage for people who have CP can be wide ranging. Massage stimulates the circulation of blood and lymph (which deals with toxins in the body), stimulates the immune system, reduces muscular tension and reduces pain in muscles and joints. A good massage can be as refreshing and relaxing as sleep, especially since muscles often remain tense even in sleep.

Certain oils have chemical constituents in them which will affect the brain and have a sedating or antidepressant effect. Many of the common problems associated with CP may be helped with aromatherapy. For example, there are oils which work against chest infection (expectorant oils which shift and loosen mucus) so it will be possible for the child to cough them up. These oils can be burnt in the room for long periods of time to keep the benefits building up. A daily stomach massage (in a clockwise direction) is one of the best ways to shift faeces around the intestines to combat constipation. Certain oils used in combination with the massage will increase its effectiveness. There are certain oils which stimulate the immune system and help children to fight off infections; some may even prevent infections if used regularly. A reputable aroma therapist or reliable book should be consulted in this regard. *The Complete Book of Essential Oils and Aromatherapy* by Valerie Ann Worwood (ISBN: 978-0-931432-82-8) and *Encylcopaedia of Essential Oils: The complete guide to the use of aromatic oils in aromatherapy, herbalism, health and well-being* by Julia Lawless (ISBN: 978-0-007145-18-8) is recommended.

## OTHER COMPLEMENTARY THERAPIES

There are very many more alternative or complementary systems available. It is not possible to detail them all but the following might also be of interest.

### Alexander technique

The Alexander technique is a form of re-education used primarily to get rid of faulty habits such as bad posture, over-tension, incorrect breathing and speech defects.

## Kinesiology

Kinesiology is the science of muscle testing to determine the interrelationship of the physiological process in the body with respect to movement. It is thought that kinesiology may be able to detect energy imbalance before many other tests.

## Spiritual healing

Spiritual healing is concerned with the transfer of energy from healer to patient. This energy is known as 'prana' or universal life force for which the healer acts as a channel.

## Yoga

Yoga is a self-help exercise and meditation system which can help to reduce stress and relieve muscle tension, as well as contributing to all round fitness.

# Chapter 9

# INFORMAL SUPPORT, SOCIAL FACTORS AND DISADVANTAGE

## FRIENDS AND FAMILY

### Friends

A number of mothers talked to me of the loneliness they experienced following the birth of their children. This can happen whether or not your child has a disability but, for mothers whose children do have disabilities, the isolation is accentuated by many factors.

Friends may be fearful that your needs as a mother will be beyond the scope of what they feel able to give. They may avoid you rather than talking to you about your situation. Friends who have the best intentions in the world are not immune from society's negative images of disability. They may feel afraid of disability, unable to know how to communicate and tend to steer clear of the situation rather than face it. The first they may hear is that there is something 'wrong' with your child, probably well before they actually see you again following the birth or diagnosis. This will allow plenty of time for wild imaginations to run riot from the starting point of *'wrong'*.

Friends can also be your best source of strength in those early days when you are adjusting. Friends may really want to support you and share your experiences but they may need your guidance on how to go about it. The best way to get support from your friends is to ask for specific things which are quantifiable in both time and effort. If your friends know exactly where they stand and what is required of them, they will be more likely to enjoy the experience and less afraid of it. Perhaps you can start by inviting them round for an informal meal and getting them to hold and play with your child while you prepare the food. Once they are used to the child (and he is used to them) they may be happy to progress on to short spells of babysitting.

## Fathers

When two parents are involved, there is real opportunity to share anxieties, work out strategies for dealing with problems and share the joys of each small success. However, many fathers can become frustrated with the sudden loss of attention from their partner and resent the intrusion of the child. This can apply whether or not your child has a disability. There is an intense learning process which takes place around having a child who has disabilities and this increases the likelihood that the father will feel pushed out. Mothers often tend to bond more quickly with children and may find it easier than fathers to make contact with their child. Fathers may experience their child's disability in a much more negative way. This is hardly surprising in a world where there are constant images of 'perfection' which we are all meant to strive for and which men are expected to uphold and procreate. The sense of failure can be overwhelming for a father. There are proportionately more families with a disabled member that are single parent families than those without. A survey carried out by Contact a Family in 2003 found that almost one-quarter of the respondents feel that having a child with a disability has caused major problems in their relationship or has even led to their separation and that over one in six of the respondents are bringing up their disabled child alone (Acton. Shapiro and Contact a Family 2004).

## Siblings

Brothers and sisters play a very important role in the life of a child who has disabilities and vice versa. There are two distinct ways this can develop with a variety of overlap in between. First, an older brother or sister can be a protective and caring friend to the young sibling. Second, the older child may experience jealousy and isolation when a lot of energy and attention appear to be concentrated on a sibling who might not even seem to respond very much. However, children often expect less from others anyway. I have seen many a situation where the disability of another child doesn't even register while the parent of the non-disabled child is plainly uncomfortable. We can learn a lot from children in this respect. I have seen older brothers and sisters quite happily interacting with their younger brothers and sisters who have disabilities without even considering that they are in any way 'different'.

Make the most of every opportunity to involve older children in your child's life and development. Over-protection is a temptation that needs to be avoided where possible. Children with disabilities need to feel that they have a life outside of their disabilities. Older children need to feel that they are still loved and valued. Trusting them with your smaller child is one way to do this. It is often easier with younger siblings as they have no sense of missing out. To them it is a normal part of life to grow up with an older, disabled brother or sister and you need to foster this from the word go.

## Extra problems encountered by single parents

An enormous burden is placed on the single parent. Not only do you have the job of nurturing your child and facilitating her development, but also you are responsible for bringing in the financial resources to enable the family to survive. Being a single parent is challenge enough by itself without the extra responsibility of bringing up a child who has disabilities which need to be confronted. Extra help is available to single parents; unfortunately you may have to go out and seek it but it *is* there if you know where to go. Voluntary groups, parent support groups and social services should be at your disposal. Make sure that you use whatever facilities are available in your area. There may be a helpline for carers and/or people who have CP in your local area. Your local library should have information. A sympathetic social worker may be able to put you in touch with voluntary and statutory assistance.

## Extra problems encountered by families with more than one disabled member

Twin births which have complications or are premature run a higher risk of one or both children developing cerebral palsy. If both are affected it is unlikely that it will be to the same degree. Also, having one child with a disability is no guarantee that subsequent children will not be disabled (although it is statistically unlikely).

Each individual responds differently to their circumstances. The problems experienced by the parents of more than one child with disabilities will be similar to those of carers of one child with a disability but the issues will all become intensified. Coping ability is likely to be stretched to the limit and the psychological trauma more severe. Transport can be more difficult to arrange. The possibility of becoming isolated and housebound increases. Financial problems are likely to be severe. On top of this there will be a double schedule of treatment and therapy to accommodate.

It is especially important for carers of more than one child who have disabilities to get access to relief and support. Respite care, home help, help with care in the home, benefits and grants should all be utilized. You should ensure that you are referred to a social worker who can channel every available means of support to you – ask your GP or health visitor about this.

## Child abuse

Studies have suggested that children with disabilities are up to ten times more likely to suffer from abuse than children without disabilities. This link has statistics for the deaf population: www.nctsn.org/sites/default/files/assets/pdfs/FactsonTraumaandDeafChildren.pdf and this one links to facts about abuse of the population of children who have disabilities: www.nctsn.org/sites/default/files/assets/pdfs/traumatic_stress_developmental_disabilities_final.pdf (National Child Traumatic Stress Network, 2012). It has also been shown that the number decreases when the child is taught to sign and thereby given early communication. A disproportionate number of children with disabilities are likely to be victims of some form of abuse (the two main forms of child abuse are those involving violence and sex). The highest levels of abuse have been found to take place in residential homes. However, there is a higher than average level of abuse within the parental home as well.

The dividing line between discipline and violence may seem thin at times. If you are a parent of a child who has problems communicating, and maybe cries a lot as a result of her frustration, you may find it difficult to restrain yourself from hitting out at her – especially if you are worn out with sleepless nights and prolonged crying. The fact is, however, that children with limited mobility or who lack a means to communicate effectively are extremely vulnerable. They are in even less of a position than their non-disabled peers to hit back, shout out or run away. If you feel like hitting your child, it would be kinder to leave the room even if it does mean leaving her on her own screaming her head off. If you need to get your aggression out, hit a pillow – *hard*. If you fear that you are unable to contain yourself there are help lines you can ring. In the UK the Scope Cerebral Palsy Helpline is geared to give support in this area, as are Parents Anonymous and CRY-SIS. Pick up that phone before you hit out at your child.

As with physical violence, sexual abuse of children with disabilities may be more common because of the child's inability to report what is happening. Non-disabled children who are abused often fail to report what is happening because they are afraid of losing the only security they know or because they are afraid of reprisals. If you suspect that your child, or a child you know, might be a victim of abuse, in the UK call NSPCC Childline 0800 1111. To get help or report abuse in the US or Canada call the Childhelp National Child Abuse Hotline at 1 800 4 A CHILD (1 800 422 4453). In Australia call the Child Abuse Prevention Service: 1800 688 009 and in New Zealand call Kidsline: 0800 543 754 or visit ChiWorld.org for a list of other international child helplines.

## THE HOME ENVIRONMENT

A human being's basic needs are for food, rest, warmth and shelter. In addition to these are a host of emotional and intellectual needs which are necessarily met by direct interaction with others be it spoken, felt, or seen and heard as through reading or music. Most of us take the basic needs totally for granted, but many people with disabilities cannot. Severity of disability will affect the extent to which a disabled person is dependent on others, but there are often ways of reducing the dependence.

There are basically two issues which should be considered in giving a person with disabilities full opportunity for living independently in the home. These are:

- housing design

- support within the home.

### Housing design

The way in which your accommodation is designed can make a significant contribution towards your independence in the home. Architects and providers of housing are beginning to realize the importance of accessible design for people with disabilities and new legislation is making the provision of appropriate adaptations easier to access.

The two main types of self-contained dwelling construction for people with disabilities are mobility housing and wheelchair housing. For those who need extra support, shared housing (sometimes with a live-in warden) is a possibility.

MOBILITY HOUSING

Mobility housing is built to normal space standards but includes features such as ramped entrance, wide doors, mechanical access to upper room (either by lift or stair lift) and bedrooms and bathrooms on the ground floor. These standards are designed to meet the needs of people who can walk a little but who may need to use a wheelchair some of the time.

WHEELCHAIR HOUSING

Wheelchair housing is designed especially for people who are permanently confined to a wheelchair or use a wheelchair most of the time. Special consideration will be given to the ground level on approach to the property, internal planning to allow a wheelchair to manoeuvre, doorways of a width to ensure easy passage of a wheelchair, kitchen and bathroom planning to allow for use from a wheelchair, switches and door and window handles placed appropriately for operation from a wheelchair.

DESIGN CONSIDERATIONS AND ADAPTATIONS

Considerations in design include the following:

- Doorways and hallways should be wide enough for wheelchairs.

- Ramps should be used instead of steps.

- Stair lifts should be installed where steps are unavoidable.

- Sinks, cookers and other kitchen appliances should be within easy reach with handles that are easy to operate.

- Windows should be easy to open.

- Plugs, switches and sockets need to be within easy reach.

- Easy access to gardens is important.

- Space standards in bathrooms must allow for wheelchair access.

- Hoists may be needed to help with bathing and getting the person in and out of bed.

- Heating should be adequate and easily controlled.

- Good insulation should be installed.

- Toilets may need to be adapted so that the user can be independent if at all possible.

If your home needs adaptations, or if you feel you need to relocate to another house in order to have a properly accessible home, your first point of contact will probably be the local housing department. Some housing departments employ access officers who specialize in accessible design. Another good source of support in the UK is housing associations, especially those who specialize in housing people with disabilities (National Housing Federation, see the Useful Addresses and Contacts section). An occupational therapist will normally become involved in helping to organize the home for maximum independence.

There are a number of organizations which offer advice on adaptations to the home, as well as on equipment which can be installed in the home to facilitate independent living. In the UK the Disabled Living Foundation keep a comprehensive collection of aids and appliances, equipment and design criteria which can be viewed by appointment.

THE ENVIRONMENT OUTSIDE THE HOME

In the UK, under the Disability Discrimination Act (DDA) 2004, service providers will have to make 'reasonable adjustments' to the physical features of their premises to overcome physical barriers to access. Similar legislation exists in a number of other countries.

A 'physical feature' is defined as including the following:

- any feature arising from the design or construction of a building on the premises occupied by the service provider

- any feature on those premises of any approach to, exit from or access to such a building

- any fixtures, fittings, furnishings, furniture, equipment or materials in or on such premises

- any fixtures, fittings, furnishings, furniture, equipment or materials brought onto premises (other than those occupied by or on behalf of the service provider) in the course of (and for the purpose of) providing services to the public

- any other physical element or quality of land comprised in the premises occupied by the service provider.

## Support within the home

Support that can be provided under statutory provision will vary from place to place and country to country but might include home helps, laundry service, meals on wheels and district nurses or care assistants.

HOME HELPS

Social services can provide domestic and other help (such as help with shopping) through the home help service. The service is not sufficient to provide full independence to a severely disabled person but can be a useful back-up to other services.

LAUNDRY SERVICE

A laundry service can be provided by social services but there may be a charge depending on the family's income.

MEALS ON WHEELS

Volunteers deliver meals to your home organized by the local authority. There may be a charge for the service.

DISTRICT NURSES OR CARE ASSISTANTS

The health authority may employ trained nurses or care assistants to pay regular visits to provide domestic health care such as help getting in and out of bed and bathing. Referrals are usually through your GP.

## Residential accommodation

The inability of families to maintain provision of care has been found to be the major precipitating factor leading to a person with disabilities entering residential accommodation, the most common problems being parental ill health or death. Traditionally residential care has tended to be medically based, with the resident with a disability being expected to assume the role of 'sick' person. Times are slowly changing and there is a move among providers of residential settings to try to develop more along the group homes lines, providing people with disabilities with as much independence as is possible. Unfortunately, however, large numbers of traditional residential units do still exist where residents (whether or not they will it) live in a state of total dependence on staff.

There have been developments since the 1980s towards supporting people to live in group homes that more nearly resemble a normal home situation, with ideals such as the following:

- That every person with cerebral palsy has the right to self-determination.

- That every person with cerebral palsy should have the option of having his own accommodation.

- That every person with cerebral palsy should be assisted to use community facilities if he chooses to do so.

- That every person with cerebral palsy should be given the opportunity to learn new skills.

- That the key investment of service provision should not be in large, institutionalized buildings, but in people providing appropriate assistance.

- That every person with cerebral palsy has the right to share equally in the benefits and difficulties of life in the community and should be encouraged to participate in the mainstream of community life as much as possible.

The concept that people with disabilities should be able to 'live an ordinary life' is gaining strength internationally.

## PERSON-CENTRED PLANNING

Based on the principles of inclusion and the social model of disability, person-centred planning is a structured process in which someone, usually called the focus person, is helped in making key decisions about their own life. John O'Brien, Jack Pearpoint and Marsha Forrest are credited with developing the approach in North America during the 1970s and 1980s (O'Brien and O'Brien 2000). They began by working in institutions where people with disabilities were living and experiencing a need for a more inclusive setting.

The focus person and other key figures they choose attend meetings to explore various goals and develop a plan for the future. Some successful examples of person-centred planning include the following vignettes:

- A young adult with a disability lived independently but did not have many friends or opportunities to go out and socialize in the local community. Bringing together some acquaintances from his local church group for a Planning Alternative Tomorrows with Hope (PATH) changed this by making some specific plans for regular get-togethers. A PATH is a meeting where friends and other people who love and care for the individuals with a disability meet with them to help them decide on their medium-term goals in life and work with them to see what is practical and possible to enable them to be realized.

- Two teaching assistants attending a training course expressed concern about their ability to support a pupil with a disability at their school. A solution circle was used to tease out the problem and look for solutions. A solution circle is a half-hour meeting where one person poses the problem while the others in the group listen. Then the rest of the group propose solutions while the problem poser listens. There follows a discussion and the activity culminates in the development of a set of actions that will be taken immediately.

- A young man who has cerebral palsy was due to attend a mainstream secondary school which had not included a student with his type of impairment before. A person-centred approach enabled him to meet with family and key people from his primary and secondary schools to discuss hopes and fears in an honest way which was kept positive by the process.

- A young man who has autism was attending a mainstream school and felt socially isolated. A circle of support was developed by asking the students in his class if anyone would like to meet once a week for 15 minutes to offer support and to keep the momentum going.

Meetings don't have to be long. They usually take between two and four hours, though longer meetings are sometimes organized around a shared lunch.

## The aim of the person-centred plan

Person-centred planning aims to support the focus person by realizing five dimensions of inclusion:

1.   Belonging.

2.   Sharing places.

3.   Being somebody.

4.   Making choices.

5.   Making a contribution.

There are five themes of person-centred planning:

1.   Creating a vision for the future.

2.   Sharing resources.

3.   Building the community.

4.   Developing support.

5.   Creating capacity.

There are five prerequisites for a person-centred plan:

1.   *Everyone involved continue listening and learning from each other.* Suspending judgement while listening to new ideas, learning from what others have achieved, raised expectations with every success and making adjustments that respond to the changes in people's lives are all part of the process.

2.   *Family members and friends are full partners.* The participation of the people who know and love the focus person is vital. They may have important knowledge about the focus person that can help service providers. Even where family and focus person have lost touch or where there is concern around safety these conflicts can be negotiated so that the person gets the support they need.

3.  *The focus person is at the centre.* The person needs to be listened to whatever their means of communication. It might mean that the people involved in the plan need to take time to get to know the person so that they can develop effective communication.

4.  *Hopeful action.* The goal of a person-centred plan is that a person with a disability or a person with learning difficulties takes an equal place in their community. Historically there has been negative reaction to the full inclusion of people with disabilities in society. Person-centred planning is a positive approach that puts practical plans in place to ensure that the focus people can realistically work towards their goals.

5.  *Developing capacity.* Person-centred planning identifies and celebrates the gifts and abilities of the focus person and insists that they make a full contribution to their community. Being able to make a contribution is central to developing a sense of self-worth. The process needs to ensure that the focus person's contribution is recognized. This contribution might involve just being in a situation that requires a new and different approach. It might involve a skill that the focus person has that the person-centred approach can draw out and develop.

It is important that notes are taken at person-centred planning meetings and there is a very specific format for note taking. It requires that you place a very large piece of paper on a wall and draw shaped outlines for each section of the meeting. The conclusions of each section are then written into the relevant shape with illustrative drawings wherever possible. The use of multicoloured marker pens aids this process. Use the yellow pen to draft your shaped outlines in advance. Person-centred planning meetings should be supported by two facilitators, a process facilitator and a graphic facilitator or illustrator. The process facilitator's job is threefold:

1.  *Listen deeply.* Facilitators must not bring their own beliefs or attitudes into the discussion. They need to faithfully mirror what is said and seek clarification without judgement.

2.  *Hold the question.* This involves keeping those present mindful of the questions that the group needs to focus on to move the process forward in a positive way. The deeper questions at the base of all person-centred planning are 'What gifts does this person have?', 'How can we make the person's gifts flourish?', 'How do they contribute?', 'How can we support that contribution?'

3.  *Support agreements.* The meeting needs to conclude with a clear, practical, realistic action plan which everyone present signs up to. The facilitator needs to ensure that there is an action plan with people signed up to do what they said they would by a certain date.

The graphic facilitator writes and draws. To do the graphics properly you need a very large sheet of paper that is fixed to a wall. The key discussion points and conclusions are written up with illustrations where possible to keep a record of the meeting. They do not bring their own beliefs and attitudes into the process and are unlikely to talk during the meeting other than to clarify a point for noting. There are set designs for each tool. There are some good examples of illustrations on the Inclusive Solutions website at www.inclusive-solutions.com and at www.helensandersonassociates.co.uk/.

The concept of a person-centred approach is beginning to gain ground in statutory services with attempts taking place to provide services within this framework. If this is not readily available in your area, ask for it.

## OUTSIDE THE HOME
### Childcare

Getting decent childcare is a problem for carers who wish or need to work when their children are small. Even as the children grow older, school hours do not fit in with most working hours. Facilities which are sometimes available on school premises for after school care are less likely to be available for children who have disabilities. In addition, you will probably want a quality of care which ensures that your child's special needs are being catered for adequately while you are at work. Specially trained nannies are hard to come by and expensive. Au pairs are unlikely to have training (although enthusiasm can go a long way) and you need the extra space to house them as well as money to pay them. Childminders can be a good option but you will need to satisfy yourself that the childminder you choose is keen to facilitate your child's development. Nurseries may offer priority to children who have disabilities but, again, you need to be satisfied that they are geared up to meet your child's needs. Catering for your child's needs in a group setting does not necessarily mean that your child must be provided with special toys, particular attention or physical therapy. Attitude is just as important as all of these. A good childminder or nursery worker will be able to integrate your child by encouraging non-disabled peers to lose sight of any sense of 'difference' that they perceive in your child.

In some areas there are nurseries and under-fives facilities which cater specifically for children with disabilities but their existence does not guarantee you a place or that your child will be cared for according to your wishes. Seek advice from your local authority or social services. Your local cerebral palsy centre may be able to offer advice.

Whatever form of childcare you choose, you will need to ensure that the people caring for your child are keen, interested and positive in their approach. You will also need to make sure that they are well acquainted with your child's particular needs, interests and method of communication.

## Everyday life out in the community

Your everyday life is affected by a great many factors. Family, friends, education, where you live, who you socialize with, your beliefs, your financial position, your employment situation, the amount of free time you have to yourself and your independence (physical or emotional) all play their part. For this reason it is not possible for any guidebook to give advice which applies to everyone on participation in the community. There are some generalizations, however, which might apply to most people who have disabilities. Parents of children who have visible disabilities may feel embarrassed about these and tend to shy away from taking their children out in public. Attitudes are changing slowly but this continues to be an issue for many parents. If the reason is not embarrassment, the sheer difficulty of getting around might put parents off taking their children out and about. A vicious circle then emerges in which people with visible disabilities are viewed with suspicion and fear because so few of them get out into the world. This in turn contributes to embarrassment or fear on the part of parents, or even the person herself. Another common occurrence is the misplaced sympathetic gesture: strangers coming up and offering you or your child money, for example saying 'Aah, the poor little thing'.

There are no easy ways of combating unwanted attitudes from the public. It is certain, though, that hiding children who have disabilities away at home will only serve to perpetuate misguided and negative images. If people with disabilities were more visible and active in the community we would eventually see a breaking down of the barriers.

It is often the way that, where discrimination exists, it is the people who suffer the discrimination who make the first move towards creating a shift in public opinion. Parent support groups can be helpful too. Parents working together with disabled adults are able to form pressure groups and lobby for changes in the environment such as ramps and disabled toilets in public places, to make access to the community easier or improve integration in mainstream playgroups and schools. Schools themselves can help by putting on shows and events which include positive images around disability. The same considerations should apply to the design of public buildings as in the organization or adaptation of the home.

## RACE, CLASS AND DISABILITY

Middle-class, articulate parents are well placed to tap into services which are available for children who have disabilities. However, parents from under-privileged backgrounds or those who do not speak English as their first language may not even get into the system, let alone reap any benefits from it. Parents often have to discover for themselves what their entitlements are to services and benefits. Those parents who are used to bureaucracy, or even have perhaps worked within the system, are bound to find the process of discovery easier than those whose cultural or class background differs.

Professionals have said to me, 'The resources are there for everyone but "they" don't come forward'. The onus often gets placed on the person who is having difficulties with the system in the first place to make the effort. There may be many reasons why people do not come forward to take advantage of services. Professionals can and often do go a long way towards redressing these imbalances by making the effort themselves to ensure that they explain to clients precisely what they are able to offer in language that is easy to understand. Physiotherapists and doctors, for example, should avoid using jargon and should clearly explain the purpose of certain exercises and treatments, etc. Social workers and health visitors need to ensure that clients are aware of the statutory services and benefits to which they are entitled. It would help enormously if professionals such as health visitors could carry application forms for standard benefits around with them to hand out to clients. There should also be someone in health service employment who ensures that clients are put in touch with local and national voluntary agencies and charities who can offer support. Information sheets and leaflets should be translated into languages which are commonly used by local ethnic groups.

An even more complex issue than access to information and services is that of expectations and attitudes held by professionals. Racial discrimination and discrimination against people with disabilities have some parallels. Traditionally non-white people have been expected to integrate into British society and to turn their backs on their own systems and cultures. This is bound to lead to failure. You cannot expect a person to become someone different, and the attempt to force such changes on people from other cultures negates them and threatens the loss of the wealth of new experience which can be offered to the host culture. Similarly, people with disabilities are expected to strive to forsake their differences and to refashion themselves into a non-disabled mould. Not only is this impossible but also it negates the positive contribution that people with disabilities, just as they are, can make to society. Professionals and non-disabled people need to see the person first. Legislation can help to guard against overt discrimination in society but only willingness and effort from members of society who do not experience disadvantage is going to change the more covert discrimination expressed in negative attitudes and dismissal of the worth of people who are perceived as 'different'.

A person who is black and has a disability is up against double discrimination. He may experience isolation in groups of white people with disabilities or in groups of black, non-disabled people. He will be especially likely, therefore, to come up against prejudice. Publications addressing this issue are beginning to be produced and pressure groups are forming (see the Useful Addresses and Contacts section).

## Gays and lesbians with disabilities

Discrimination against gays and lesbians may operate in a slightly different way in that sexual orientation is not generally visible. It depends on the individuals whether they wish to be known as gay or lesbian. However, an enormous amount of prejudice exists against gays and lesbians. If you have a disability and are open about your sexuality there may be a fear that you are more vulnerable to abuse or attack than a non-disabled gay person.

If you want to enjoy meeting others in the gay community and your mobility is restricted, your choice about being open about your sexuality may be limited. It's a bit difficult for a gay person to get a parent to phone Dial-a-Ride (a taxi service for people with disabilities operating in London, UK) to enable him to attend a gay function without being open about his sexual preference.

There are no easy answers to these problems but supportive family and friends are essential for gay and lesbian people who have disabilities to enable them to enjoy a full life and have access to the lifestyle of their choice. Local gay organizations may be able to offer some advice (see the Useful Addresses and Contacts section).

## Local, informal support groups

There will be some self-help support groups in most areas. In the UK, your local branch of Scope and the town hall should have a list of the local groups. Support groups can work in a number of ways. Groups of parents who get together and identify common needs can often prove to be a powerful force in campaigning for improved services, introducing new ideas into a community and even setting up resource centres themselves. Some groups may provide opportunities for parents to meet and discuss feelings and needs. Other groups might form with the specific purpose of increasing services to children via self-help (under parental control). In London, a group of parents came together in the late 1980s to start a play and learn group for children with disabilities. We called the group PALACE (Play and Learn and Creative Education) and our aim was to prepare our children to enter mainstream education, give them opportunities for social integration and interaction with non-disabled children and complement local authority therapy with input from a Peto-trained physiotherapist. We also involve volunteers in playing with our children while parents get together for discussions. This gives parents a break, allows children to build up relationships outside the family and offers valuable experience to the volunteers. Another group of local parents (whose children had recently left school with nowhere to go) came together to create a facility for their children (based at a local community centre) which aims to create individual programmes for the young adults involved so that they can continue to develop and enjoy a social life in the community. Both of these groups are still offering services over 20 years later.

Groups such as these are being or have been set up in many places, but finding out about them isn't always easy. Local branches of the larger disability organizations may be able to help. The health professionals who come to see your child will often have heard of local groups.

## FUNDRAISING

Resources cost money and not all will be available through social or educational services. While some argue that needs should all be met by statutory services, the hard facts are that not all necessarily will. However, if you come across equipment or treatment that you feel would be of benefit to your child it is wise to find out whether funding can be made available from the local authority before you embark on a strenuous fundraising exercise. Examples of the things for which you might wish to raise funds include the following:

- Therapy treatments which are not generally available in your country or not contained within your health service (such as patterning and conductive education).

- Setting up or running costs for support groups and self-help groups.

- Equipment such as computers, non-standard seating, video cameras (to facilitate progress monitoring), non-standard wheelchairs and walking frames, seating and buggies, adapted toys and learning aids.

There is a lobby in the Disability Rights Movement which strongly objects to fundraising by donation (particularly the popular television events). There are a number of sound reasons for these objections:

- Reliance on charity detracts from the fact that people with disabilities have a right to services and equipment which meet their needs to enable them to participate equally in society.

- It perpetuates the idea that people with disabilities are somehow inadequate.

- It encourages people to sympathize and contribute due to guilt rather than to recognize the equal worth of people with disabilities.

- Giving donations may lead people to believe that they have in some way 'discharged their duty' where disability is concerned.

- With charitable funding the distribution of resources becomes very uneven. Only those projects and individuals who 'know the system' are likely to get access to charity.

- There is still not enough money available through these sources to really meet need.

The real need is for a change in attitude and for funding to be channelled to ensure that equal rights are automatically available to all people with disabilities.

Ironically, it would probably be cheaper, in the long run, if a concerted effort were made to produce environmental adaptations and ensure equal rights implementation, instead of relying on the rather piecemeal funding which is currently available. Having said all this, if you really feel the need for some specific equipment or group activity, using charitable funding is one way of possibly gaining access to it. If you cannot get funding from the local authority the next step is to contact appropriate charities who may be able to offer grants. (Your local library should have a list of grant-making trusts.)

If all else fails you might wish to consider a fundraising effort organized by yourself or by local people. Sponsored events are the most popular, such as sponsored runs, swims, bike rides, dances (anything). Other ways to raise funds privately include market stalls, raffles, stalls at Christmas or summer fêtes and collecting boxes in cafés, pubs or shops. It should be remembered that these events often involve a lot of effort for very little financial reward, but they may tip the balance to enable you to purchase much needed equipment or services. I recently came across a simple and easy to organize method of raising money which might be of interest. If you ask 10 people to find 10 people each who would be willing to donate £10, you will raise £1000. To make this effective it is a good idea to produce an information sheet (with a photo on it if possible) so that the collectors can show this to people they are requesting donations from.

To give fundraising legitimacy it is preferable for you to be collecting money under a registered charity number. There are some organizations who will act as an 'umbrella' for individuals wishing to raise money to meet their children's special needs. Alternatively, you can get together with other parents or individually set up a charity. Setting up a charity is not easy and you would be advised to seek an easier option than setting up an individual charity for one child. Group efforts are often more successful than lone activity.

When you are raising money you need to be fairly careful how you phrase information about what the money is being raised for. If you specify a very narrow option for spending the money and then find that the facility you are raising money for is no longer available, you may be legally barred from using the money to serve other needs your child may have. On the other hand, it is imperative that money is spent on activities or items which would be considered charitable. When raising money for Dan I usually either specify a range of options for which the money will be used or make a general statement that the money raised will be used to benefit his development.

Chapter 10

# EDUCATION

## 'LEAST DANGEROUS ASSUMPTION'

Nicholas is 16 years old and has severe disabilities. He is not able to speak, he uses a wheelchair to get around, and has some visual impairment. The team is not certain as to what Nicholas understands or how aware he is of his environment. Should Nicholas be fully included in regular high school classes?

### SCENARIO 1

We assume that Nicholas cannot understand and is not aware of his environment so we keep him out of most regular high school classes. Ten years later, we discover that we were wrong and Nicholas does understand and is aware of his environment. What have we lost?

### SCENARIO 2

We assume that Nicholas can understand and is aware of his environment and we fully include him in all typical high school classes, with relevant supports and high expectations. Ten years later, we discover that we were wrong and that Nicholas is not aware of his environment and does not understand. What have we lost?

## THE VALUE OF EDUCATION

Education is the cornerstone of our future lives. It is the key which opens the door to all future possibilities. Everything we are able to do as adults is the result of what we learnt as children. This includes the value we put upon ourselves as human beings as well as our social standing and ability to be financially and domestically independent and to fulfil our ambitions. The kind of education we receive can empower or disempower depending on where we are taught, what we are taught, by whom we are taught and with what end in view.

It is important to consider what needs a child will have as an adult, when he is being entered into the education system. This is especially so if the child has a disability. If you are aiming only to give your child social and domestic independence and not giving consideration to academic achievement, then his chances of obtaining gainful and rewarding employment are limited. If you consider only the child's academic opportunities then chances of independent living might be limited.

## PRE-SCHOOL LEARNING

Pre-school learning opportunities are particularly helpful to children who have disabilities, and local authorities have a statutory obligation to consider the special educational needs of children with disabilities who are under the age of five years.

Whatever the extent of your child's disabilities, he will be helped by a little extra preparation before entering full-time education. There are a number of statutory options which might be available in your area. Alternatively you can find out about pre-school learning and spend some time preparing your child yourself. Another option is to get together with other parents who have pre-school children and gather mutual support in offering your children pre-school opportunities.

### Pre-school nurseries

There is a fairly short supply of pre-school nursery places available in the UK. Availability of places varies from area to area. Your local education authority should be able to advise you about which institutions to approach. Nurseries are sometimes attached to primary schools and it is worth considering entering your child in a nursery at a school he is likely to attend long term if at all possible. Some nurseries operate separately from local schools. Many of these are funded by the local authority although there has been a recent increase in the number of privately run nurseries. If your child is recognized as having special educational needs at an early age, you may be entitled to high priority for a nursery placement. Your local social services or education department will be able to advise you about this.

### Preparing at home

Peripatetic teachers are available in some areas but they are unfortunately in short supply. Ask your education department if they can offer you this facility. The local educational psychologist may also be able to offer advice on this. Peripatetic teachers who are trained in special education can visit on a regular basis and offer advice on how best to prepare your child for full-time education. Some teachers use specific training programmes, such as Portage (see below), for children with disabilities. Some teachers may specialize in hearing or visual impairment, or both.

### Portage early education programme

Portage is a system for assessing the needs of young people who have developmental delay and then teaching them the skills they need to acquire. It is a home-centred system which involves regular home visits from a member of the MDT running the service. The home visit provides an opportunity for parents to seek guidance, discuss needs and set learning targets for this child. The parent is recognized as the key figure in a child's development and the Portage system is designed to help parents to focus on their child's abilities and learning needs and carry out tasks which will aid his progress.

### Mother and toddler groups

Find out if there is a local mother and toddler group your child can attend with you. This will give him an early chance to interact with non-disabled children and to learn from group play activities.

## CONDUCTIVE EDUCATION

Conductive education is a pre-school and school age learning system especially designed for children with motor impairment and aims to given them the opportunity to enter normal school with the effects of their disability reduced.

### Background to conductive education

The main aim of conductive education is to produce *orthofunction* (ability to satisfy biological and social demands) in children with motor disorders so that they can take up places in Hungarian general or special schools. However, it is a system which is receiving unprecedented publicity with a huge lobby of parents pushing for its swift introduction in Britain. The system was devised in Hungary during the 1950s by Andras Peto (a physician who specialized in institutions of rehabilitation). Conductive education was devised in a very different culture where the demands of the education system and the economic climate vary greatly from the UK. The importance of being able to walk is emphasized because, under the Hungarian education system, children who are unable to walk cannot attend either a general or a special school. For these children teaching tends to be home based, which is unsatisfactory and costly. Conductive education is not a long-term alternative to meet the educational needs of children who are otherwise unable to manage in the general school system. It specifically aims to remediate motor and other learning difficulties experienced by certain groups of children with the aim of discharging them into the general school system.

Peto set up a National Institute for Kinesitherapy in 1950. Kinesitherapy is the treatment of disease by means of passive and active movements such as massage and exercise. By 1963 the institute had become the Institute for Training of Educators of the Locomotor Handicapped and the Educational Home for the Locomotor Handicapped. It was here that he began training conductors in the system which is used today.

After Peto's death in 1967, Dr Mari Hari took over as director of the institute, a position she still holds today. A new institute has now been established in Budapest since 1985 and is called the Andras Peto Institute for Motor Disorders. Since 1963, the Peto Institute has provided a statutory service for all school children in Hungary who have disorders for which conductive education is felt to be an appropriate remedial method.

There has been wide criticism of the method – mainly due to lack of scientific data, research papers or general written work from Hungary to enable the system to be evaluated. However, it is generally acknowledged as being successful in creating 'orthofunction' in pupils who attend.

Ester Cotton (a physiotherapist who was working for Scope) provided the initial force in developing conductive education in the UK. Inspired by the work of the Peto Institute she produced a system of pre-school motor training designed to enable young children to acquire 'basic motor patterns' essential for full physical function. Her system is not conductive education but used techniques found within conductive education under the influence of a conductive philosophy.

In 1992 Scope reached an agreement with the Peto Institute in Hungary. Initial assessments for British children are now available at various conductive education inspired learning environments. Hungarian conductors often work at the centre as well as British ones.

There are a number of independent centres internationally which aim to offer techniques inspired by conductive education. See the Useful Addresses and Contacts section. Some of these centres are employing Peto trained conductors. There are also some conductors working independently.

In 1984 the Birmingham Institute for Conductive Education was formed. The Birmingham Institute aims to bring conductive education into the UK in a systematized way which will enable, as near as possible, a true replication of the work of the Peto Institute in the UK. In 1987 ten trainee conductors, all of them holding British teaching qualifications, were recruited. At the same time ten children, all of whom have cerebral palsy, were selected with the help of two Hungarian conductors to be the first intake into the Birmingham Institute. The children and trainee conductors spend part of their time working in the UK under the direction of Hungarian conductors and part of their time working in Hungary. Further children continue to be assessed and trainee conductors recruited as the work of the Birmingham Institute expands. A second institute has been developed in Scotland called the Scottish Centre for Children with Motor Impairments.

Some of SCOPE's schools have focused on conductive education. In the USA conductive education is supported by the Inter-American Conductive Education Association. There are a number of conductive education centres in Australia (see Useful Addresses and Contacts section). The original centre in Budapest is now known as the Peto Institute (see Useful Addresses and Contacts section).

## How is a conductive education programme carried out?

Andras Peto considered motor disorder as a learning difficulty to be overcome rather than a condition which requires treatment or accommodation. He set out to establish motor function in young children which would diminish or eradicate physical handicap which might otherwise persist into adult life. It is also intended that overcoming motor disorder through an integrated learning programme will facilitate the child in all aspects of development (e.g. intellectual function and personality development). Conductive education has been found to be helpful to children and adults with a number of 'conditions' which involve motor dysfunction. These include cerebral palsy, spina bifida, stroke and Parkinson's disease.

It is the educational emphasis of the system which sets it apart from other methods which have been devised to help children who have cerebral palsy in their development. The context is a learning one in which children use their own efforts to overcome their problems under the guidance of a trained conductor. The will and determination of the pupil play a central role in the success of the system and the training is designed to take place within the wider context of a general education system for all.

Another important aspect of conductive education is that almost all of the learning takes place in groups. Children are matched in groups and learn together. Each child's achievements are noted and appreciated by the group as a whole. In addition to the incentive of group support, development is aided by the example set by the achievements of peers.

Motivation is important and devices are employed to aid the development of motivation through song, rhyme, the use of toys, etc. as well as highlighting the achievements of children who have done well and giving appreciation to other children and conductors.

Children who attend the Peto Institute go through an intensive day during which every activity of daily life is an opportunity for education. Those who are resident at the institute begin their day by being woken by a conductor who will help them with dressing and toilet before breakfast. Independence is the ultimate goal of every task. Where children require assistance from a conductor this is kept to a minimum and the children may also help each other in basic tasks such as dressing. Slatted benches are used for most activities (such as dressing, washing and eating) as the slats in the bench maximize self-help, enabling the children to steady themselves and retain balance. At about 9 a.m. children will begin the daily routine of 'lessons' generally known as 'task series'. Task series teach the performance of tasks learned spontaneously by healthy children. They are neither simple exercises nor defined anatomical movements but intentional activities in a biological sense. These might include sitting, grasping and other hand control activities, and ultimately standing and walking. The children learn in a group and demonstrate their intention verbally. For example, the child may say 'I stretch my right hand back' while the conductor aids the child to undertake the task. The next part of the task might be 'I stretch it down again', and so on, culminating in 'I clap my hands'. Day by day the level of achievement required by the schedule rises. Task series represent the path which is seen to lead to orthofunction. They are goal directed and carefully constructed to meet the function needs of the specific group of individuals undertaking them. Task series learning is interspersed with 'conditioning' (e.g. toilet training, washing, eating, etc.) The process continues up until lights out at 9 p.m.

## Criticisms of the system: positive and negative aspects

There have been many criticisms of conductive education made by therapists who operate from different traditions. These include the following:

- The system is exclusive, only taking children who have demonstrated certain intellectual and physical abilities prior to training. The success rate is only so high because of the 'weeding out' of more severely disabled children in the early stages.

- The high demands of the training are too great for small children to cope with.

- Reliance on one professional to facilitate all aspects of a child's development can only lead to a less skilled professional in individual areas of development such as speech.

I have met adults with cerebral palsy who heavily criticize conductive education for detracting from the real issues of the need for better access in society and improved provision of aids and adaptations. They also criticize the regime as cruel and yet another attempt to force the person with disabilities to fit into society rather than society adapting. This is a long-standing dilemma and conflict which will continue to surround the issue of provision for people with disabilities. There is no easy solution and I do not intend to propose one in this publication. I would only suggest that every person who has disabilities deserves the right of access to whatever form of support may be available and desired by that person to facilitate their equal and full participation in the community.

## ENTERING YOUR CHILD INTO THE GENERAL EDUCATION SYSTEM

### Making a choice about your child's education

If your child is only mildly affected it is unlikely that he will require a statement or individualized programme and you will probably choose to send him to a local mainstream school in the normal way. However, the majority of children with cerebral palsy are likely to have some special educational needs and it is important that you are clear about your choice of education for your child as early as possible so that appropriate arrangements can be made for his needs to be met successfully.

In the UK the main choices are currently between special schools, mainstream schools and special units in mainstream schools, although mainstream placements are becoming the preferred option by authorities and families as world-wide recognition of the need for inclusion gains ground. Teachers in mainstream schools are beginning to prepare themselves for a changing role through training and in-school discussion. A very useful document 'The Index for Inclusion' has been produced by the Centre for Studies on Inclusive Education (CSIE) and distributed to all schools in the UK by the Department for Education. This document guides schools through a process that will help them to better understand the value of inclusive education.

In the USA the Individuals with Disabilities Education Act ('IDEA') 2004 gives students with disabilities the right to be educated alongside non-disabled students in the general classroom. In the UK the Education Act 1996 provided a similar right for students with disabilities. This has been further strengthened by the DDA 2005, which amended the Act of the same name from 1995. Under the DDA educational establishments must make reasonable adjustments to enable students with disabilities to attend. They also have a duty to promote equality of opportunity. Legislation in individual countries is further supported by more global legislation such as the United Nations Convention on the Rights of People with Disabilities to which many nations have subscribed. This legislation provides that all people with disabilities should enjoy full and equal enjoyment of all human rights and fundamental freedoms which promote respect for their inherent dignity. Full participation and inclusion in society along with respect for the evolving capacities of children with disabilities who have a right to preserve their identities are enshrines as two of the eight guiding principles of the UN Convention. The shift from medical to a social model thinking is explicit in the convention. Of particular relevance to education is Article 24, which provides that all children with disabilities should participate in a state education system that should be inclusive at all levels.

## Special schools

It is important that the place of special schooling is seen in its historical context. In the UK special schools were set up, mainly in the 1970s, in response to new legislation which gave all children with disabilities the right to receive education for the first time in history. Previously, children with disabilities had managed to cope, without extra support, in ordinary schools, or they were sent away to 'caring' institutions or they had been kept at home by families who did their best for their children in whatever way they could. Initially then, the opportunity to go off to school, albeit a special one, seemed like a great step forward. However, we are now left with a legacy from these schools which has proved to be the great educational dilemma for children with disabilities in the 1990s and beyond. The distinction between education and therapy must be understood and recognized. The special school system tends to mesh these two needs together, often prioritizing therapy over education to the detriment of academic outcome. The specialist curriculum often focuses on independence skills rather than academic ones.

Some special schools are boarding schools and, in many cases, the special schools recommended for your child will be outside the local area. The distances children have to travel and the lack of contact with their peers in the local community which travelling to a special school produces are two of the many arguments which are levelled against special school provision. Other arguments include the following:

- Special school education is essentially segregated education. Children are kept away from their local community and educated among other children who have special educational needs. Every child who has a disability is a unique individual so the grouping together of children with disabilities does not necessarily ensure that your child will be receiving an education which is better suited to her needs than that which is available at a local mainstream school.

- The environment of the special school is very separate from that of the general community. Sooner or later your child will be expected to take a full part in her local community. A child who has been kept in a segregated community until the age of 19 is ill equipped to deal with the outside world.

- Specialist schools may tend to underestimate a child's abilities and it is possible that education will be tailored more towards domestic and social skills than towards academic achievement.

Arguments in favour of special schooling usually go along the following lines:

- Resources being concentrated in one place enable a child to have more ready access to other services. For example, most special schools will have physiotherapy departments and regular input from other relevant health professionals. (I have also, however, heard many parents of children who attend special schools complain bitterly that they feel their children do not receive sufficient time and attention from the school health service and that their own involvement in their child's health care is diminished by the concentration of therapeutic activities within the school.) Also, with new legislation mainstream schools will increasingly become aware of this need.

- Special schools are meant to be readily equipped with aids and adaptations as well as specialized teaching equipment and specially trained teachers.

## Mainstream schools

The successful enjoyment your child will have of education at mainstream schools will depend on a number of factors. The extent of your child's disability and the amount of 'extra' help he is likely to need will be of prime concern to the school. If your child's disability is mild with little or no extra help needed, the main concern is likely to be the attitudes of non-disabled peers and teachers towards him. Because disability is still so hidden in our society it is an unfortunate fact that negative images pervade in society. Cruel remarks and bullying from other children can become a common occurrence. However, children do not behave in this way spontaneously. They learn such behaviour from adults and images around them in society. A positive attitude from teachers (and particularly head teachers) can do much to overcome this. So can contact with and support from other parents. People with disabilities will not avoid the pain of negative attitudes from others by being hidden away. It is only by full and continued participation in society, coupled with positive legislation, that attitudes can be made to change.

If your child's disability is severe it will probably be necessary for you to obtain a statement of his needs or an individualized educational plan so that proper provision can be made within the mainstream setting. It is possible for the local services to provide your child with an assistant in school, or more than one assistant if necessary, to enable him to have his physical needs met and to aid him in carrying out lessons.

There are various theories on the best way to enable inclusion. My own position is that inclusion begins at birth. If children with disabilities are invited and encouraged to take a full place in society from the start of their lives there is no reason to suppose that they will not be able to take their place beside non-disabled peers in all walks of life and all activities.

In order for a mainstream school to be able to offer full educational opportunities to children who have special educational needs it is essential that staff are prepared and trained to be enablers for these pupils. If you are considering a mainstream school you should talk to the head about the attitude of the school towards children with disabilities and find out if there are any teachers who have relevant training in special needs. It will be particularly important that the class teacher responsible for your child is keen, and that she is made fully aware of your child's needs, method of communicating (especially if he uses signing or an electronic communication system), etc.

We all hope that our children will be able to keep up with their peers and fully participate in the curriculum. However, if your child has severe disabilities or takes a little longer to learn than some others, you might have to discuss ways of enabling him to benefit from appropriate education without losing out on activities where he can fully join in with his peers.

The success of placing your child in mainstream schooling will depend on a positive partnership between parents, child, peers, teachers and the local education authority. They should all be working together to ensure that proper planning takes place prior to your child entering school and that you meet regularly throughout his schooling to review progress. Schools are required to appoint a teacher and a governor who have specific responsibility for special educational needs.

Arguments against placing a child in mainstream education include the following:

- Parents fear that their children are more vulnerable than others and will not be able to cope with the rough and tumble of school life.

- Children with disabilities can become isolated in mainstream schools because they may not be able to keep up with peers.

- Mainstream schools are not properly equipped to deal with special needs.

- Other children might pick out a child who has disabilities for derision and bullying.

In general legislation specifically sets out to counter these problems. It is my own experience, having worked in many segregated and inclusive settings, that attitudes and commitment are far more important than provision made in legislative frameworks.

Arguments in favour of placing a child in mainstream education include the following:

- A mainstream environment enables children with disabilities to grow up to understand and accept the real world in which they live.

- Mainstream education offers an opportunity for better academic achievement than many special schools are able to provide.

- A child in mainstream education is more likely to be educated alongside friends from the local community with whom he can develop out-of-school relationships.

- Mixing disabled and non-disabled pupils will help to break down barriers which might otherwise lead to those without disabilities having negative attitudes and fear around disability when they grow up.

## Special units in mainstream schools

The compromise option of special units in mainstream schools has been popular in some areas. By having special units, it is intended that children with disabilities can benefit from social interaction with non-disabled peers and share some lessons with them. Time can also be set aside, within the special unit, for education to focus on the special educational needs which children with disabilities might have.

In practice, the school has to take great care to avoid children in special units becoming isolated in just the same way as they might if removed to a special school. There is still segregation in this practice.

# OTHER OPTIONS

## Special schools linking with mainstream schools

Many special schools form links with local mainstream schools and groups of children can visit between schools for specific sessions. This system is quite often adopted for pupils in special schools who, it is felt, should be slowly integrated into a mainstream setting where they will eventually attend full time.

Unfortunately, part-time can be as little as 1–3 hours per week and the child with a disability is often only invited to participate in non-academic curriculum activities. Members of the inclusive education movement are strongly opposed to these arrangements arguing that they only offer a glimpse into another world for the child with a disability and no real participation. It has been contended by the movement that this kind of integration is about as realistic as calling someone 'a little bit pregnant': you either are or you are not! It can also be extremely disruptive as the child with a disability does not know which community she is meant to belong to and which curriculum she is meant to follow.

## Educating your child other than at school

If you are unable to find a suitable school for your child, educating her at home or getting together with other parents who feel similarly dissatisfied with the provision on offer may be a real alternative. Home schooling is an option in most countries but the amount of support you can expect to receive varies from one place to another.

In the UK there is a movement of parents who prefer their children (many of whom are not disabled) to be taught at home. More information can be obtained by contacting Education Otherwise (see the Useful Addresses and Contacts section).

Another organization known as the Human Scale Education Movement is keen to promote the idea of education as a lifelong process of development of the whole person, helping people to grow, not only in knowledge and skills, but also in health, feeling, judgement, sense of responsibility and creativity (see the Useful Addresses and Contacts section). The movement is particularly focused on three initiatives as follows:

- Mini schools and other schemes which allow large-scale schools to restructure on a human scale.

- Small schools, especially where the intention is that they should be non-fee paying and have open access; the challenge is to provide a wide curriculum and high adult/pupil ratio without being 'uneconomical'.

- Flexi-schooling, which encourages schools to combine school with home-based or community-based education.

The Human Scale Education Movement is keen to encourage new initiatives and support parents and teachers working for change in the mainstream.

## Private education

There are a number of private educational establishments with very different philosophies.

Steiner schools have an educational theory which differs from the UK state education system. They believe in drawing out a child's creative abilities and imagination and do not press children to learn academically until they reach the age of seven. There are a number of Steiner boarding schools which have been set up specifically to cater for children with special educational needs. Some of these schools have enabled children to make enormous progress in social and emotional development in cases where they have suffered deprivation in these areas. Steiner schools use art and music extensively.

If you are interested in Steiner schools, see the Useful Addresses and Contacts section to find out more.

Ordinary public schools usually have very specific entrance requirements and you would need to talk to the school in question to find out if it would consider accepting your child and on what basis.

The Montessori system was devised to cater for children with special educational needs. The teaching system is very intensive. Each child's development is individually supported with carefully graded and sequenced learning strategies. Over time the majority of Montessori schools have become mainstream schools and the same issues face children with disabilities entering a Montessori school as those facing children with disabilities entering an ordinary mainstream school. In addition to this the parents will have to find fees.

## MAKING THE DECISION

Now that parents are much more enabled than ever before to decide to educate their children with disabilities in mainstream schools, and these schools are becoming aware of their duty to provide for the needs of every individual child, it should only be necessary for parents to look at other alternatives if they have a specific goal in mind that they really don't feel a mainstream school can make provision for. Even so, do talk to your local mainstream school, or your nearest designated school before you make any decisions.

## EDUCATIONAL PROGRAMMES FOR STUDENTS WITH CEREBRAL PALSY

Recent research is suggesting that we can teach literacy (and by that I mean reading and writing words made up of letters of the alphabet) to many more people than was ever believed possible.

Thanks to the work of Karen Erickson, Caroline Musselwhite and others we can now up the stakes in special and mainstream settings where children with learning and/or communication difficulties are being taught. Both Karen Erickson and Caroline Musselwhite (www.aacinternetion.com/) have developed schemes to support the process (Erickson 2000; Musselwhite 2011). It may be that materials need to be differentiated to make them accessible but there is no reason why the starting point should not be the same for everyone.

Local mainstream schools are beginning to develop the skills to differentiate the ordinary curriculum rather than develop special ones. I have had some really positive experiences in special schools where we have worked together to ensure that the curriculum is expanded to include academic options that stretch the young people in their care in addition to independence skills training. Without literacy the rest of the curriculum will be very hard to tackle. Without literacy it will be very difficult for the person with a disability who has communication difficulties to get across everything they want to say.

I have taught literacy in many different ways. In one special school we found that a young autistic man was able to acquire word recognition through his extreme fascination with Thomas the Tank Engine. He learnt to recognize the words 'Fat Controller' and 'Percy' and eventually went on to begin to generalize the skills learnt to more generally useful words.

Patricia Logan Oelwein (1995) explains that teaching reading to children with what was then called 'moderate retardation' was virtually non-existent in the 1960s. Her wonderful book, *Teaching Reading to Children with Down Syndrome: A Guide for Parents and Teachers*, is packed with guidance on teaching reading to young people who have Down syndrome. Near the beginning of the book she relates a story that I feel is very important when we are thinking about attitudes and the power of our expectations. She tells of a mainstream teacher who had a couple of children with Down syndrome join her class. She had never had any training in how to work with students who had special needs so she set about teaching them to read as she did all the other students in her class and they did learn to read. To her consternation she was advised on a training course that she later attended that children with Down syndrome could not learn to read. She had to inform the course tutor that she did not know any better so she just taught them to read. This incident took place a long time ago. Today there is a general acknowledgement that children with Down syndrome should have literacy instruction and that many will be able to read and write. People with Down syndrome now have university degrees, pass their driving test, have sexual relationships and can generally live ordinary lives. This was thought to be impossible in the mid 1900s. Now there has not been a change in the nature and make of people who have Down syndrome. What has changed is society's attitude towards people who have Down syndrome and teachers expectations of what they might be able to achieve.

One thing is certain. A child who is not exposed to literacy will find it difficult to acquire literacy skills.

# Chapter 11

# AFTER SCHOOL – WHAT NEXT?

'What happens next?' is a question which plagues the vast majority of children nearing the time when they leave school and enter the adult world. There is a vast wealth of choice on the surface but, with the increasing demand in the employment market for higher educational qualifications and/or experience, these choices are becoming more limited. Choices include studying for a degree or vocational qualification, going on a youth training scheme if you lack the exam results for higher education, going straight into the workplace in an unskilled position, unemployment or marriage and/or raising families.

As well as how to earn a living, other questions likely to beset a child prior to leaving school include: 'Where will I live when I leave home?' 'Who will I live with?' 'How will my sexual and emotional needs be met?' Special interests and hobbies are often already developed by the time a child leaves school but not always so, and this can be another area for concern at this important time in every person's life.

Before we go on to look at the particular way in which these issues might affect an emerging adult who has cerebral palsy, I would like you to jot down your answers to the following questions. These questions may be hard for you to answer but I urge you to make every effort to do so. Only by taking on such a task can you begin to know what children with disabilities face as they emerge into the adult world.

- Did you leave school with a clear idea of what career you wanted to follow? Please write down details of your experience in this respect.

- Did you follow through with the same career or did your choice change as time went on and how?

- How did the things you learned at school connect with your subsequent life path or career?

- Did you feel confused about your sexuality? In what ways?

- Were there problems in deciding how and when to settle down with the partner of your choice? What sort of problems did you encounter?

- Did you feel afraid about your future security? Why?

- Did you feel the need both to be with your parents and away from them at the same time? Why?

My guess is that you will have found it difficult, if not painful, to look at the issues raised in answering these questions. Add to this a world which assumes that you are virtually incapable of contributing to the job market before you even get a chance to prove yourself, which does not consider that you can have valid, emotional, sexual or security needs, and consider where this would leave you at the age of 16–21!

I'm going to suggest that we are asking a bit too much to expect an emerging adult with disabilities to slot neatly into an often prescribed adult role when most of us left school feeling fairly shaky about our chosen path.

## OPTIONS FOR SCHOOL LEAVERS WHO HAVE DISABILITIES

Theoretically, school leavers who have disabilities have broadly similar options to those who do not have disabilities. These options fall into the following categories:

- Further education:
  - attending university
  - attending local further education (FE) establishments
  - studying at home (distance learning).

- Economic options:
  - FE or training
  - employment (full-time or part-time)
  - unemployment
  - home-based activities (including home-making and working from home).

- Living situation options:
  - staying at home with parents
  - settling down with a partner
  - living independently in your own home
  - living in a community setting.
- Social options:
  - finding or having a peer group to share entertainment with
  - expanding and building on non-work interests (hobbies, etc.)
  - broadening your solitary entertainment (reading, listening to music, watching television, etc.)
  - having sexual experiences.

It is impossible to generalize about the way in which these options will present different obstacles for young adults who have cerebral palsy. It is important to remember that they are all likely to be obstacles in some way or another for anyone. The young adult with CP is, however, likely to have extra hurdles to leap over while finding their way into adult life and there are a number of institutions and services which might be able to help make the passage easier.


## FURTHER EDUCATION

All young people have a legal right to education until their nineteenth birthday in the UK. This may vary in other countries. Many stay on at school, transfer to another school or enter a local or residential college.

There are two traditional FE paths. The first is to move from secondary school to a sixth form centre (unless the secondary school has its own sixth form) so that study can begin for advanced examinations which would enable entrance to university or to study vocational courses. In the USA the transition is to senior high school. The second path is attendance at an appropriate institution for training in vocational skills. This enables students to acquire competence-based qualifications. In the UK there are National Vocational Qualifications (NVQs), Scottish Vocational Qualifications (SVQs), national diplomas or other similar qualifications.

There are a number of qualifications that have been developed in the UK to enable students with learning difficulties to gain a qualification such as the Certificate of Achievement. These qualifications allow young people who would not be able to gain the same level of qualification as their peers to still receive a certificate acknowledging the skills that they have.

A bright teenager with severe physical disabilities, with the aid of technology, should be able to access higher level qualifications, for example, in management provided the will of the employer is apparent. In the UK the DDA provides for more positive opportunities as employers will be expected to make reasonable adjustments to enabled disabled employees to participate.

In some areas pupils can attend 'link courses' at a local FE college while they are still attending school for one or two days per week. Link courses are particularly useful for students who are considered to have moderate learning difficulties.

There are assessment centres which are intended to help people with disabilities to find out what their capabilities are and make realistic plans for the future. In addition, a number of mainstream colleges and universities offer facilities to aid independence in a mainstream setting.

The teenager with a disability is likely to encounter extra obstacles and be required to put in much more effort than a non-disabled peer just to be able to go to a FE establishment. Special arrangements may have to be made for examinations (which you need to know about and apply for in advance). An example of the piecemeal way in which integration is attempted was demonstrated by one London college which carefully geared up its computer department for wheelchair access and was disappointed to find that the opportunity was not taken up by any wheelchair users. The college had failed to take account of the transport difficulties that students with disabilities might have, and there were no disabled toilets in the building. This kind of anomaly should be reduced with the implementation of the DDA.

The choice between specialized or mainstream FE is likely to be heavily influenced by how much social independence has been achieved by the student. Specialist institutions will offer courses on independent living and social skills as well as vocational or academic training. However, there have been criticisms made that some specialist institutions put too much emphasis on social skills and not enough on academic skills.

## The Open University and other distance learning institutions

The Open University and similar institutions offer home-based FE with special facilities for students with disabilities. It offers a wide range of courses which can lead to the obtaining of a full degree or certificates which will enhance work opportunities. The system is designed to cater for students who are not able to study full-time and you can therefore spread your degree course over a number of years while building up skills and confidence in other areas or undertaking employment.

If you are continuing in education in the UK, your benefits should not be disrupted unless you are attending residential establishments, in which case your Disability Living Allowance might be affected. You might only be able to claim Disability Living Allowance for the periods you are actually at home. Students may qualify for an Educational Maintenance Allowance if their parents' income is very low.

## FINDING WORK

In employment, as in every other aspect of life, the person with a disability has the added disadvantage of negative attitudes to contend with. In 1986 a study into discrimination in employment against people with disabilities was commissioned by Scope and undertaken by Eileen Fry. The method employed was very simple. Employers' responses to two (fictitious) letters of application, which differed only in that one was from an applicant with a disability and the other was not, were analysed. In 41 per cent of cases the applicants with disabilities received a negative response while non-disabled applicants received a positive one. In only 3 per cent of cases was the reverse true. There were examples in the study of non-disabled people being asked to interview while applicants with disabilities with exactly the same qualifications were not. In some cases applicants with disabilities were informed that the position had been filled while the non-disabled applicant was invited to interview.

There are a number of schemes to help people with disabilities to get an ordinary job. In the UK job centres employ disablement resettlement officers who are taught to discuss alternatives and the careers service employs specialist careers officers.

There are a number of employment services available to people with disabilities.

### Self-employment

Self-employment is becoming an increasingly popular way to earn a living and may have particular attractions for the adult who has disabilities in that the problems of transport and availability of disabled facilities (such as toilets) are avoided. However, working for yourself often involves long hours and has the disadvantage that workplace training opportunities are not available. In addition to this the self-employed person has to take responsibility for his own tax and National Insurance payments.

## Incentives for businesses to employ people with disabilities

In the UK there are a number of incentives available to encourage firms to employ people with disabilities.

Government schemes exist to support disabled people in obtaining work and managing in work. You can find out the current schemes available in the UK at this website: www.direct.gov.uk/en/DisabledPeople/Employmentsupport/index.htm

The Employers Forum on Disability offers helpful advice to employers as well as statistical information about disability and employment across a range of countries. You can find them on this website: www.realising-potential.org/. Support for US citizens can be found on the US Department of Labor website at: www.dol.gov/odep/.

In Australia the Department of Human Services has information at this link: www.centrelink.gov.au/internet/internet.nsf/services/disability_emp_services.htm

## Volunteers and paid assistants in the workplace

There are numerous schemes that supply either volunteer or paid support assistants to enable people with disabilities to carry out their jobs. In the UK there is a rise in the direct payments and individual budget schemes which enables adults to receive an allowance to appoint staff and other support so that they can enjoy an ordinary life. You can ask your local social services whether such a scheme exists in your area.

## Considerations for people with disabilities in mainstream employment

There are a wide variety of positions which can be filled by people with even severe disabilities provided that access to the place of employment is arranged and specialist equipment is available where necessary.

The advent of computer technology has made the office environment much more accessible for people with disabilities and there is a wide range of courses available to enable people with disabilities to develop their computer skills. In addition, there are many computer accessories now available which can enable even a severely disabled person with restricted limb movement to manage a computer system competently. Telephone systems can be adapted for those who might have difficulty with an ordinary telephone mouthpiece. Employers may be surprised to find how efficient and able employees with disabilities can be as their motivation to achieve and to prove themselves is likely to be high.

One of the cleanest and most efficient office environments I have had contact with was the Islington Disablement Association in London, which I had occasion to visit for advice on benefits as well as for help with research for this book. There is a fairly high percentage of employees who have disabilities. I was given coffee while I waited, all my queries were answered (or appropriate advice given on where to go for more information) and the organization was quick to send me fairly bulky photocopied information which I requested. I came away feeling that employers who have reservations about taking on people with disabilities would learn a lot from a visit to this office and perhaps clear away some of their prejudice.

It is noticeable that the organizations who lead the way in having good employment practices are those which actually cater for the needs of people with disabilities. Even in these organizations, however, there are very few people with disabilities who have senior positions. Basically this comes back to education. Unless students with disabilities are given a real opportunity to gain qualifications and appropriate training, there will always be an inequality in higher management positions. The only way to achieve this is to offer students with disabilities the same options as those who are not disabled and to ensure that the facilities are in place to allow access to educational establishments. Although there is a lack of funding in this area, there is also a lack of awareness among employers and educators regarding the needs of people with disabilities and, often, a lack of commitment to taking the necessary steps to improve people's opportunities. All of this contributes to high unemployment among people with disabilities, and the low average among those fortunate enough to gain employment.

## Day centres

In the UK most local authorities run day centres which are establishments that open daily and offer recreational activities and assistance with improving independence for people whose disabilities are of sufficient severity to prevent them from working. Day centre workers are employed to facilitate activities and there are commonly group activities available on a regular basis. From my own experience of working in a day centre, examples of the kinds of activities available include arts and crafts, music, printing, reality orientation for elderly people with Alzheimer's disease, practice with domestic tasks, reading groups, newsletter production and similar activities. I remember one gentleman who was fairly elderly and immobile due to motor neurone disease but who had an extremely agile mind discovering an ability to invent crossword puzzles through his involvement in the newsletter we produced on a monthly basis. Planning the monthly crossword helped to restore his confidence and sense of purpose. On the other hand I also remember a teenage boy with severe cerebral palsy who attended the centre being left to sit in his wheelchair for long periods of time without stimulation. It is well worth checking out the extent of the staff's understanding of cerebral palsy and what activities they would propose to offer before recommending this option to an adult who has CP. Social services can advise on day centres in the locality.

## RELATIONSHIPS AND SEXUALITY

Forming close relationships can pose problems for people who have physical disabilities. In the first instance the problems may be those experienced by all young people growing up and becoming aware of their sexuality. Puberty is confusing for most adolescents and, over the years, the education system has taken on board the need to prepare young people for adulthood in providing sex education (albeit in an often clinical way).

However, young people with disabilities are often regarded as asexual beings. It is often assumed that they will be barred from an active sexual life and parents and educationalists often fail to recognize that the feelings and needs of an adolescent with disabilities are likely to be exactly the same as the non-disabled adolescent. In addition to this, the disabled adolescent may well develop complexes around issues of sexuality as part of a general pattern of low self-esteem, lack of confidence and lack of information.

It is *absolutely wrong* to assume that someone who has cerebral palsy has no sexual feelings or that they cannot enjoy a fulfilling sex life. It may be that they will need to discover ways to obtain full sexual enjoyment which take account of whatever physical difficulties they experience but sexual enjoyment is as much a right as any other equal opportunity issue facing an adult with disabilities.

There is an emergence of more organizations which aim specifically to support people with disabilities in forming meaningful relationships and having a satisfying sex life. A useful self-help guide for disabled people and their families is *The Ultimate Guide to Sex and Disability* (Kaufman, Silverberg and Odette 2003).

In the UK there are a number of dedicated online dating agencies at: www. disabledunited.com/, www.dating4disabled.com/, www.disabledcupid.com/, and www.disabilitymatch.co.uk/. The In Touch Project offers advice and support to young disabled people around sexuality and relationships (see Useful Addresses and Contacts section). Contact a Family have produced a useful booklet for parents which can be downloaded as a pdf at: www. cafamily.org.uk/pdfs/GrowingUpParents.pdf. The Outsider's Club supports gay and lesbian people with disabilities. Gemma is a group that supports disabled and non-disabled lesbians.

The American Association of Disabled people have a directory of disability related organizations at this link: www.access-board.gov/links/disability.htm. Disabilities are Us is a chat forum which can be accessed at: www.disabilities-r-us.com/

## SPORT AND LEISURE

There are numerous organizations and publications which concentrate on specific sport or leisure activities for people with disabilities. Direct payments and individual budgets can have provision made in them for access to leisure activities.

## INDIVIDUAL STORIES

The best way to look into a positive future for a child who has cerebral palsy is to hear some real-life stories of people with CP who are leading successful lives in an inclusive environment.

### Alan Martin

This short account of my life, so far, has been written by myself, because I consider myself the best qualified to write on this subject.

I was born in 1963 and remember little of the first few years of my life. I know that I was the second of five children, which must have been a huge challenge for my mum! I was in hospital for three and a half years, and remember there was an old red fire engine outside for the children to play on. That is my strongest childhood memory, (confirmed later in life by people who were also there and remember it!) Disturbingly, I also remember doctors talking over my head as if I couldn't understand what they were saying. I understood quite well, and it was all very negative.

After coming home from hospital, at age four years, my mum had to start the fight to get me into any school because they said I was ineducable. Chestnut Lodge in Widnes, eventually gave me a place, and I stayed there from when I was 5 to 18. In the 1960s special schools didn't have to provide an education. I was just kept happy and entertained. I played wheelchair football and did some woodwork, but never learned to read and write.

On leaving school, I was sent to a residential independent living college in Banstead, for two years, where I learned to go to the pub, and about sex, which I suppose is a big part of independent life, but not much help to earn your living! On 'graduation' I was returned home, to attend an adult social services day centre, five days a week.

At the day centre I was mainly in the company of elderly and sick people, and I was completely bored almost to death. Brains sucked out of me!

Until I was 31 I had little help with communication. I used some signs and facial expression but only people who knew me well understood. I lived with my father and step-family. I was frustrated that they made all the decisions for me and I wanted to live independently but could not tell anyone. I was very unhappy with a situation where I had no control over my own money, but was just given a little pocket money.

Years of having no choices or control in life led me to become desperate, and I ran away to London because I was frustrated and fed up after a row with my dad. The police fetched me back but I spent two days in London without any assistance. I was in a manual wheelchair and just got by with help from the public. A short multi-award winning film about this part of my life, 'This Chair is not ME' has been made by Andy Taylor Smith. It was made two years ago, and is still winning awards across the globe!

When you think about it, the basis for happiness is having control over things. Not being able to do everything for yourself but choosing what you do and who helps is vital. I'd like to emphasize that independence doesn't mean doing everything for yourself. It means having independence of mind and making your own choices.

That event led to many people realizing how unhappy I was and when I was 31 some good friends found out about electronic communication aids. Unable to get any statutory funding, they raised the money themselves to get me a communication aid. There was a problem getting sufficient training to use the aid, but I persevered and with help was able to convince the authorities to get me my own home. I had to be patient, something I am not very good at. I would not have been able to do this without the electronic speech aid! In 1994, getting my first communication aid put me in control of my life for the first time. I began to take part in society instead of just being a spectator.

The first few words and sentences I was able to express just started the ball rolling and for the first time in my life people were interested in what I had to say. During the first year of having a voice I attended dozens of meetings of many organizations and undertook many short courses. In that year I went on a Candoco Dance Company training course and this was when my interest in creative, inclusive dance began.

Over the following years my involvement with groups and organizations mushroomed almost out of control. I belonged to over 50 groups. It gave me confidence, involvement and a feeling of self-worth. I gave up my place at the day centre to some other lucky person! It was through contacts at these voluntary engagements that people wanted to start to pay for my services. This led me to think about setting up my own business.

I'm a dance workshop leader and I write my own music, also I give disability issues presentations. In 2004 I became self-employed, and gave up most of my welfare benefits. This was a scary step to take, due in some part to knowing that there was no going back once I had proved that I could work for my living. So far my business is very successful, and has developed into an organization which can also offer accessible music making to accompany creative dance, and most recently I have started workshops using light painting techniques, combined with creative dance, to produce lasting images of original and exciting light scenes which participants can have and use in any way they choose. This light painting is particularly successful done by people who use wheelchairs, as they offer many fixing points for multiple light sources.

As well as my dance practice, I work with universities around the country, on movement projects, and also on research projects to do with synthetic speech and Augmentative and Alternative Communication (AAC). It's interesting work, and helps pay the bills!

About two years after getting my first aid and getting my self-confidence I made plans to move into my own home. I faced opposition from my family as they were convinced I would not cope and would be back within days. In 1998 I moved into my own home. I've made plenty of mistakes and learnt lots from them. There have been no serious accidents and I'm fitter and healthier than ever. My bungalow was rented from a housing association, formerly the local council, and I now own it myself.

This bungalow was the first one I was shown when my social worker was trying to find me a home. It was partly adapted before I moved in. Ramps to the doors and a wheel-in shower were built. Later, more adaptations were done for me making it easier for me to move around and use my kitchen. I carried on living there through the adaptations and I don't think I'd do that again. It took longer than I expected.

I had to think carefully about who to employ for personal assistants. My social worker advised me to employ my own staff rather than rely on people from agencies. At first I employed a couple of friends. What I needed was not just 'care' and I had to make this clear. I decide what I need help with, and my staff are there to enable me to do what I want to do.

Now I have five PAs who work with me. Some have been with me for years. Having staff who know me well makes things easier. My staff are very flexible about how they work with me, and I plan my own timetable.

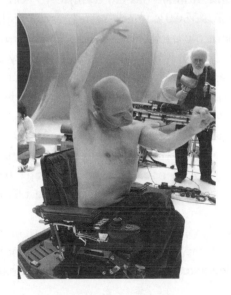

I've been lucky so far when looking for new assistants and have found people I already know or by word of mouth. Having the right attitude is more important than paper qualifications. I know people with all sorts of qualifications who are not prepared to be told by their clients or boss what he or she wants. They try to dictate and haven't lasted long.

I pay my personal assistants with money from the Independent Living Fund (ILF). The ILF has really helped to give me my independence. It is national so is not dependent on local policy. (Crazily plans to end this fund in 2015 are being considered!) I also get money from social services through direct payments. As an employer I have to make deductions from wages to pay to the tax office. At first I was given advice by the tax office, now I have software that helps me to calculate wages. My money goes further than if I used an agency because my money goes on pay and not on agency fees.

I do try to be a responsible employer because I want to keep good staff. I have had to sack people in the past and this has been very upsetting. I wrote a contract of employment saying what happens if we have problems and holiday entitlements and so on. This is one down-side of independent living for me. I hate paperwork.

When I first moved into my bungalow I owned nothing but a few clothes, an old radio and computer. Friends gave me a sideboard and bed settee. I had no carpets or fridge. I know that there are some risks to living as I do. Risk is a fact of life. We do all we can to minimize risks. So far, I and my staff have remained unscathed. We have devised ways of moving me that are safer than with lifting equipment. If I was wrapped in cotton wool, my life would be unbearable.

Getting a communication aid has led to my own home, my own staff, my own business, a role in a BBC3 comedy series, plans for the future but, most of all, the right to make my own choices. Good luck played a big part in my struggle for independence. If it had been up to statutory authorities I would have still been waiting. The TV work was very interesting, and I was very pleased to be the first genuine AAC user to be involved in a TV series. Sadly no more series followed.

My first communication aid came from fundraising by friends. My personal assistants are mainly taken from people I already know, not an agency. Other elements came purely by chance. Many people don't have this good luck factor. It shouldn't be necessary in an ideal world but it was how things worked for me.

I really love my work. I couldn't do it if I didn't. I think the most satisfying part of my business is the dance workshops. I get enormous satisfaction from the excellent feedback from adults and kids. I'd hate to give you the impression that I don't do anything in my life apart from work. Preparation and paperwork takes lots of my time. As relaxation I really enjoy writing music using computer software and I sometimes use my compositions for work. On a free day I may do some gardening or some cooking or go out in my van. I go to the theatre or to see performances by Status Quo or other bands.

My social life is pretty full and I have lots of visitors. I sometimes have my relatives staying with me and as I only have one bedroom they have to sleep on airbeds all over the place. We have a lot of fun.

I'd be a bit less free to travel to work or for social things if I didn't have my own transport. I used to use public transport and still do for trips to central London. There are still loads of issues with public transport.

People often ask me why I do so much rather than taking it easy and chilling out all day. I think I would get bored. I have many plans for the future and I am very focused. I want my own fully accessible dance studio where people can come and learn about inclusive creative dance, accessible music making, and many other creative inclusive art forms.

Life is too short to have small dreams and I have many great ambitions that are still unrealized. I really think people should have big dreams to work towards.

So my advice to you all is never let anybody tell you that you will never be able to do anything.

I plan to write my autobiography. But first I am going to write a book about dance in my life. You can keep up to date by checking out my website: www.mouseonthemove.co.uk/.

## The Road to Independence by Dan Stanton

My name is Dan Stanton. I am twenty. A year and a half ago, until which time I lived with Mum, Mick and Katie my sister, I moved into my own flat.

I have direct payments and choose my own assistants with help from my mum.

It's great to have my own place. I'd be so pleased if everybody with cerebral palsy could be so lucky although it should be your human right not luck.

I'm also out a lot on trips. I went to Windsor Castle and the proms not long ago.

I went to mainstream school until I was 16.

I don't like it when people treat me like I'm stupid and think I don't understand.

I have my own bank account and sign my name with a stamp. The passport office would not accept my stamp which I was very angry about. It is not fair that different people in powerful positions can just make up rules that make me not a person just like them.

I have used lots of different communication aids. At the moment I use a head pointer and Grid 2 software and a touch screen or the low tech spelling board. I'm hoping to try an eyebrow switch soon. I have a Dynavox but it is out of date. It has been difficult getting communication support even though Mum works with people who use communication aids.

My friends matter more than anything. I had a PATH meeting that sorted out regular times to meet. They help me to build MySpace and we are planning to write some music with me playing Soundbeam. We keep in touch on MSN and Facebook.

When I moved into my new home I had a PATH meeting. PATH works on planning positive futures helped by friends and family with someone who leads the meeting. You dream then see what is possible.

## EPILOGUE

For me these two stories give the most important information that anyone needs to have about cerebral palsy. It is possible to have an ordinary life. It is even possible to have an extraordinary life full of excitement and possibilities. Having a disability like cerebral palsy need not take this away. Our only limitations are those we put there ourselves or those that people who are prejudiced put in our way. The former we can dismiss and the latter we can challenge if we work together. There are a number of organizations led by people with disabilities who work together to challenge discrimination and promote equality. As my son was growing up I gained more inspiration from them than any of the statutory agencies.

# USEFUL ADDRESSES AND CONTACTS

## UK ORGANIZATIONS

### Organizations offering general advice and/or services to people who have cerebral palsy

**Benefits Enquiry Line**
Tel: 0800 882200
Text: 0800 243355
Email: baadmin@baadmin.demon.co.uk
Website: www.dwp.gov.uk
Northern Ireland Tel: 0800 220674, Text: 0800 243787

**Carers UK**
Ruth Pitter House, 20–25 Glasshouse Yard, London EC1 A4JT
Tel: 020 7490 8818
Umbrella organization for carers' groups offering information, contacts, advice and support for anyone caring for an elderly, sick or disabled person at home.

**Contact a Family**
170 Tottenham Court Road, London W1P 0HA
Tel: 020 7383 3555
A national charity which supports families who have children with different disabilities or special needs. It aims to help families to overcome isolation by bringing them together through local mutual support and self-help groups.

**Disablement Income Group**
PO Box 5743, Finchingfield CM7 4PW
Tel: 01371 811621
Works to improve the financial circumstances of people with disabilities.

**Family Fund Trust**
PO Box 50, Finchingfield CM7 4PW
Tel: 01904 550005
Email: acc@familyfundtrust.org.uk
Website: www.familyfundtrust.org.uk
Offers financial help and information for families with severely disabled children.

**Family Service Units**
207 Old Marylebone Road, London NW1 5QP
Tel: 020 7402 5175
Provides help for families under pressure.

**Family Welfare Association**
501–505 Kingsland Road, London E8 4AU
Tel: 020 7254 6251
Offers services and grants for families in need.

**Financial Support**
Disability Benefits Unit, Warbreck House, Warbreck Hill Road, Blackpool FY2 OYE
Tel: 0845 712 3456
Text: 0845 722 4433
Makes the decisions on claims for Disability Living Allowance.

**GEMMA**
BM Box 5700, London WC1N 3XX
Email: gemmagroup@hotmail.com

**Independent Panel for Special Education Advice**
4 Ancient House Mews, Woodbridge, Suffolk IP12 1DH
Tel: 01394 380518
Website: www.ipsea.org.uk
Provides educational advice for parents of children with special needs.

**In Touch**
Innovative Projects, Leonard Cheshire Disability, 66 South Lambeth Road, London
SW8 1RL
Tel: 08456 717 173 (local rate number)
Minicom/text phone: 0207 490 8913 extention 06
Email: innovation@lcdisability.org

**Invalid Care Allowance Unit**
Palatine House, Lancaster Road, Preston PRl 1HB
Tel: 01253 856123
Deals with claims on Invalid Care Allowance.

**Kids' Clubs Network**
Bellerive House, 3 Muirfield Crescent, London E14 9SZ
Tel: 020 7512 2112
Email: information.office@kidsclubs.co.uk
Provides information on after-school clubs and other childcare arrangements for
school-age children.

**London Boroughs Disability Resource Team**
Third Floor, Bedford House, 125–133 Camden High Street, London NW1 7JR
Tel: 020 7482 5299
Provides specialist services and expertise to enable local authorities and public
organizations to meet the needs of people with disabilities.

**National Childcare Campaign**
Daycare Trust, 4 Wild Court, London WC2B 4AU
Tel: 020 7405 5617
Provides advice on childcare services.

**National Disability Arts Forum**
Mea House, Ellison Place, Newcastle upon Tyne NE1 8XS
Tel: 0191 261 1628
Text: 0191 261 2237
Email: ndaf@ndaf.org
Website: www.ndaf.org
Focuses on promoting and supporting the development of disability arts on
national and international levels.

**Northern Ireland Information Service for Disabled People**
2 Annadale Avenue, Belfast BY7 3JH
Tel: 01232 491011

**Outsiders Club,**
4S Leroy House, 435 Essex Road, London N1 3QP
Please send a stamped addressed envelope to this address for more information.
Tel: 020 7354 8291
Email: info@outsiders.org.uk
Website: www.outsiders.org.uk/

**Palace for All**
Scholefield Road, London N19 3ES
Tel: 020 7561 1689
Provides play, alternative therapy and physiotherapy for children up to the age of
14 in London. Also runs after-school learning activities.

**PlayTrain**
The Post Office Building, 149–153 Alcester Road, Moseley, Birmingham B13 8JW
Tel: 0121 449 6665
Fax: 0121 449 8221
Website: www.playtrain.org.uk/
Provides training and consultancy for organizations working with children. Aims to increase opportunities for school-age children to be creative and express their identity.

**Project Ability**
Centre for Developmental Arts, 18 Albion Street, Glasgow Gl 1LH
Tel: 0141 552 2822
Email: info@project-ability.co.uk
Website: www.project-ability.co.uk
Specializes in creating opportunities for people with disabilities to gain access to the visual arts.

**Scope**
6 Market Road, London N7 9PW
Helpline: 0808 800 3333
Email: response@scope.org.uk
Website: www.scope.org.uk and www.scope.org.uk/help-and-information
Offers a wide range of activities to help children and adults who have cerebral palsy including advice, research, holidays, residential care, education and training, assessment, support and information, publications and videos.
Scope Response, 0808 800 3333 (as above), is a free helpline offering information, advice and initial counselling on anything associated with cerebral palsy.

**Scottish Council on Disability**
Information Department, 5 Shandwick Place, Edinburgh EH2 4RG
Tel: 0131 229 8632
Provides information to people with disabilities who are resident in Scotland and those working with them.

**Serene**
BM CRY-SIS, London WC1N 3XX
Tel: 020 7404 5011
Email: cry-sis@our-space.co.uk
Website: www.our-space.co.uk/serene.htm
Support groups for parents of crying babies.

**SNAP! Childcare Ltd**
91–93 Great Eastern Street, Shoreditch, London EC2A 3HZ
Tel: 020 7729 2200
Email: info@snapchilcare.co.uk
Website: www.snapchildcare.co.uk
Places nannies and childcare workers with children who have special needs.

**Special People**
Scholefield Road, London N19 3ES
Tel: 020 7686 0253
Fax: 020 7686 0254
Email: special.pcople@virgin.net
Website: www.specialpeople.org.uk
Provides highly qualified professionals in special needs for respite services, babysitting and nannying. Also provides teachers and therapists. A 24 hour service is available.

**Whizz-Kidz**
1 Warwick Row, London SW1E 5ER
Tel: 020 7233 6600
Email: info@whizz-kids.org.uk
Website: www.whizz-kidz.org.uk
Aims to improve the quality of life of children with disabilities in the UK and provides specialized mobility equipment such as wheelchairs and tricycles.

## Treatment and therapy

**BIRD (Brain Injury Rehabilitation Development, Centre for)**
The BIRD Centre, 131 Main Road, Broughton, Chester CH4 ONR
Tel: 01244 532047
A treatment centre employing unique approaches developed by the centre to inhibit primitive reflexes and provide for normal functional ability. The methods are relevant to the full age and severity range of brain injury victims.

**Bobath Centre (England)**
Bradbury House, 250 East End Road, London N2 8AU
Tel: 020 8444 3355
Fax: 020 8444 3399
Email: info@bobathengland.org.uk

**Bobath Centre (Scotland)**
Bradbury House, 2028 Great Western Road, Knightswood, Glasgow Gl3 2HA
Tel: 0141 950 2922
Fax: 0141 950 2933
Email: info@bobathscotland.org.uk

**Bobath Centre (Wales)**
Bobath Children's Therapy Centre, 19 Park Road, Whitchurch, Cardiff CF14 7BP
Tel: 029 2052 2600
Fax: 029 2052 1477
Email: info@bobathwales.org
Website: www.bobathwales.org/

**Brainwave**
Marsh Lane, Huntworth Gate, Bridgewater, Somerset TA6 6LQ
Tel: 01278 429089
Private clinic offering assessment and treatment based on the ideas of Doman Delacato. Aims to offer a less intensive but equally effective treatment to many similar clinics.

**British Association of Art Therapy**
24–27 White Lion Street, London N1 9PD
Tel: 020 7686 4216
Fax: 020 7837 7945
Email: info@baat.org
Professional association for art therapists.

**British Institute for Brain Damaged Children (BIBIC)**
Knowle Hall, Bridgewater, Somerset TA7 9PJ
Tel: 01278 684060
Email: info@bibic.org.uk
Website: www.bibic.org.uk/
Private centre offering assessment and treatment based on the ideas of Doman Delacato.

**British Society for Music Therapy**
69 Avonlea Avenue, East Barnet, Herts EN4 8NB
Tel: 020 8368 8879
Promotes the use of music therapy in the treatment and education of adults and children who have disabilities.

**College of Speech Therapists**
Harold Poster House, 6 Lechmere Road, London NW2 5BU
Tel: 020 7459 8521
Provides pamphlets for parents and can advise on the location of qualified speech therapists.

**Gerald Simonds Healthcare Ltd.** (Jay seating system)
9 March Place, Gatehouse Way, Aylesbury, Buckinghamshire HP19 8UA
Tel: (Free-phone) 0800 220975
International / Mobile: +44 (0)1296 380200
Email: webenquiry@gerald-simonds.co.uk
Website: www.gerald-simonds.co.uk/catalog/search_results.php?MF_ID=13

**MOVE Europe**
Unit C, 15 Bell Yard Mews, Bermondsey Street, London SE1 3TY
Tel: 0207 403 6382
Fax: 0207 403 6578
Email: move@move-europe.org.uk
Website: www.move-europe.org.uk/

**Nordoff-Robins**
Nordoff Robbins Centre, 2 Lissenden Gardens, London NW5 1PQ
Tel: 020 7267 4496
Email: musicservices@nordoff-robbins.org.uk
Website: www.nordoff-robbins.org.uk/

**Rifton Disability Equipment**
Darvell Brightling Road, Robertsbridge, East Sussex TN32 5DR
Tel: 01304 843701

**Soundbeam and Vibro Acoustics**
Soundbeam Project, Unit 3, Highbury Villas, St Michaels Hill, Bristol BS2 8BY
Tel: 0117 923 7075
Fax: 0117 970 6241
Email: mark@soundbeam.co.uk
Website: www.soundbeam.co.uk

## Communication and aids to daily living

### Communication Advice Centre
Musgrave Park Hospital, Stockman's Lane, Belfast BY9 7JB
Tel: 01232 669501, ext. 561
A centre specially staffed and equipped with many of the aids available to help
patients with communication disorders offering practical demonstrations and
individual advice on specific problems.

**David Hart**
Thorncliffe House, Dawson Road, Keighley, West Yorkshire BD21 5PH
Tel: 01535 667306
Fax: 01535 608306
At this centre children can be assessed for the use of the David Hart Walker and an after care service is available to ensure that the walker is adapted as necessary with the child's growth.

**Disabled Living Foundation (DLF)**
380–384 Harrow Road, London W9 2HU
Tel: 020 7289 6111
Works to find non-medical solutions to the daily living problems facing disabled people of all ages. The DLF's main activities are research and information provision.

**G. & S. Smirthwaite**
16 Daneheath Business Park, Heathfield, Newton Abbot, Devon TQ12 6TL
Tel: 01626 835552
Suppliers of aids and equipment.

**Quality Enabling Devices Ltd**
Riverside Court, Huddersfield Road, Delph, Oldham OL3 5FZ
Tel: 01457 819790
Fax: 01457 819799
Email: inclusive@inclusive.co.uk

**REMAP**
Hazeldene, Ightham, Sevenoaks, Kent TN15 9AD
Tel: 01732 883818
Email: john.wright@remap.org.uk
Website: www.remap.org.uk
Offers engineering help for people with disabilities by making one-off aids for individuals whose needs cannot be met by standard commercial aids or appliances.

**Scottish Centre of Technology for the Communication Impaired**
WESTMARC, Southern General Hospital, 1345 Govan Road, Glasgow G51 4TF
Tel: 0141 201 2619
Fax: 0141 201 2618
Email:enquiries@acipscotland.org.uk
Website: www.acipscotland.org.uk/index.html
Provides Scotland-wise assessments, training and information for professionals and participates in research and development in communication difficulty and technology.

**Talking Mats Centre**
2 Beta Centre, Stirling University Innovation Park, Stirling FK9 4NF
Tel: 01786 479511
Email: info@talkingmats.com
Website: www.talkingmats.com/

## Help to access Alternative and Augmentative Communication (ACC)

**Ace Centre Advisory Trust**
92 Windmill Road, Headington, Oxford OX3 7DR
Tel: 01865 759800
Email: info@ace-centre.org.uk
Website: www.ace-centre.org.uk
Offers assessment for communication aids in the southern half of England.

**ACE Centre North**
Hollinwood Business Centre, Albert Street, Hollinwood, Oldham OL8 3QL
Tel: 0161 358 0151
Fax: 0161 358 0152
Email: areeves@ace-north.org.uk
Offers assessment for communication aids in the northern half of England.

**Call Centre**
Communication Aids for Language and Learning, University of Edinburgh, Paterson's Land, Holyrood Road, Edinburgh EH8 8AQ
Tel: 0131 651 6235, 0131 651 6236
Email: call.centre@ed.ac.uk
Website: www.callcentre.education.ed.ac.uk
Provides a range of services for people with communication disabilities.

**Communication and Learning Enterprises (CandLE) Limited**
Suite 205, Ulverston Business Centre, 25 New Market Street, Ulverston, Cumbria LA12 7LQ
Tel: 01229 585173
Email: info@candleaac.com
Website: www.candleaac.com
Offers assessment and advice for communication and learning needs nationally.
Specializing in using AAC to access literacy and the curriculum and also in
supporting students with complex needs in both special and mainstream schools.

**Makaton Charity**
31 Firwood Drive, Camberley, Surrey GU15 3QD
Tel: 01276 61390
Email: Mvdp@makaton.org
Website: www.makaton.org
Provides a wide range of resources for parents, carers and professionals. They help children and adults with severe communication and learning disabilities.

**1 Voice**
255 Bolton Road, Aspull, Wigan WN2 1QR
Tel: 01422 341578
Email: Tamsinjam@aol.com
Provides information and support for children and families who use communication aids.

Many more assessment centres and other organizations that can help with AAC can be found at the following links:
www.communicationmatters.org.uk/resources
www.ace-north.org.uk
www.checkthemap.org/

## Support with aids to daily living

**Disabled Living Centres Council**
Redbank House, 4 St Chad's Street, Manchester M8 8QA
Tel: 0161 832 3678
Email: info@disabledliving.co.uk
Website: www.disabledliving.co.uk
Offers advice on all aspects of independent living.

**Mobility Advice and Vehicle Information Service (MAVIS)**
Macadam Avenue, Old Wokingham Road, Crowthorne, Berkshire RG45 6XD
Tel: 01344 661000
Email: mavis@detr.gov.uk
Website: www.mobility-unit.detr.gov.uk/mavis.htm
Offers advice on finding the best car or adaptation to suit your child's needs.

**Mobility Centre**
Queen Elizabeth's Foundation, Damson Way, Foundation Drive, Carshalton, Surrey SM5 4NR
Tel: 020 8770 1151
Email: info@mobility-qe.com
Website: www.qefd.org
Provides a free information service on all aspects of personal mobility for drivers, passengers and wheelchair users.

## Alternative and complementary treatments

### Association of Reflexologists
5 Fore Street, Taunton, Somerset TA1 1HX
Tel: 01823 351010

### British Acupuncture Association and Register
63 Jeddo Road, London W12 9HQ
Tel: 020 8735 0400

### British Homeopathic Association
Hahnemann House 29 Park Street West, Luton LU1 3BE
Tel: 01582 408675
Fax: 01582 723032
Email: info@britishhomeopathic.org

### General Council and Register of Osteopaths
Osteopathy House, 176 Tower Bridge Road, London SE1 3LU
Tel: 020 7357 6655

### Herbal Medicine Association
PO Box 583, Exeter EX1 9GX
Tel: 0845 680 1134
Email: secretary@bhma.info

### International Federation of Aromatherapists
20A The Mall, Ealing Broadway, London W5 2PJ
Website: www.ifaroma.org/

### Tisserand Aromatherapy Institute
10 Victoria Grove, Second Avenue, Hove, East Sussex BN3 2LJ
Tel: 10273 206640
Can advise on training courses and weekend seminars and has a list of qualified therapists.

## Respite

### Crossroads Care
10 Regents Place, Rugby, Warwickshire CV21 2PJ
Tel: 0845 450 0350
Provides practical help for limited periods for families with a disabled member.

## Legal advice

### Action against Medical Accidents
44 High Street, Croydon, Surrey CR0 1YB
(Please note: no unarranged callers are admitted)
Tel: 020 8688 9555 (Please note this is for administration only. For help and advice please use the Helpline below)
Fax: 020 8667 9065
Helpline: 0845 123 23 52

### Disability Law Service
39–45 Cavell Street, London E1 2BP
Tel: 020 7791 9800
Text: 020 7791 9801
Email: advice@dls.org.uk
Website: www.dls.org.uk
Provides legal advice and representation to people with disabilities and their families and/or carers.

## Education

### Advisory Centre for Education (ACE)
1c Aberdeen Studios, 22 Highbury Grove, London N5 2DQ
Tel: 020 7704 3370
Email: enquiries@ace-ed.org.uk
Website: www.ace-ed.org.uk
A registered charity offering free advice, service and publications for parents with a focus on school years (5–18) in local education authority schools only. It can advise on many questions parents might have about their children's educational rights and publishes very useful and easy to read guides to the law in this area.

### Alliance for Inclusive Education
36 Brixton Road, London SW9 7AA
Tel: 0207 737 6030

### Centre for Studies on Inclusive Education (CSIE)
The Park Centre, Daventry Road, Knowle, Bristol BS4 1DQ
Tel: 0117 353 3150
Fax: 0117 353 3151
Email: admin@csie.org.uk
Produces publications, organizes seminars and offers training on issues relating to inclusive education.

### Education Otherwise
PO Box 3761, Swindon, Wiltshire SN2 9GT
Tel: 0845 478 6345
Supporting people who wish to educate their children other than at school.

**Hornsey Centre for Children Learning**
26A Dukes Avenue, Muswell Hill, London N10 2PT
Tel: 020 8444 7241, 020 8444 8242
A centre offering early education programmes based on conductive education.

**Human Scale Education Movement**
Human Scale Education Movement, Unit 8, Fairseat Farm, Chew Stoke,
Bristol BS40 8XF
Human Scale Education Movement, London Policy Desk, CAN Mezzanine,
49–51 East Road, London N1 6AH
Tel: 01275 332516
Email: info@hse.org.uk
Website: www.hse.org.uk/
The human scale education movement advocates for small learning environments
for children.

**National Association for Special Educational Needs**
NASEN House, Amber Business Village, Amber Close, Amington, Tamworth,
Staffordshire B77 4RP
Tel: 01827 311500
Email: welcome@nasen.org.uk
Website: www.nasen.org.uk
Promotes the interests of those with exceptional learning needs and/or disabilities.

**National Institute of Conductive Education**
National Institute of Conductive Education, Cannon Hill House, Russell Road,
Moseley, Birmingham B13 8RD
Tel: 0121 442 5556
Website: www.conductive-education.org.uk/
An organization providing conductive education in the UK, replicating the
methods taught at the Peto Institute in Hungary. Also has further information on
conductive education in other parts of the UK.

**Parents for Inclusion**
336 Brixton Road, London SW9 7AA
Tel: 020 7738 3888 (office number)
Helpline: 0800 652 3145 (freephone)

**Queen Elizabeth's Foundation for the Disabled**
Leatherhead Court, Woodlands Road, Leatherhead, Surrey KT22 0BN
Tel: 01372 841100
There are four centres which provide assessment, further education, vocational
training, residential sheltered work, holidays and convalescence.

**Scottish Centre for Children with Motor Impairments**
The Craighalbert Centre, 1 Craighalbert Way, Cumbernauld G68 0LS
Tel: 01236 456100
Email: sccmi@craighalbert.org.uk

**Steiner Waldorf Schools Fellowship Ltd**
11 Church Street, Stourbridge DY8 1LT
Tel: 0 1384 374116
Fax: 01384 374142
E-mail: admin@steinerwaldorf.org

**World of Inclusion**
Unit 4X, Leroy House, 436 Essex Road, London N1 3QP
Email: richardrieser@worldofinclusion.com
Provides training and support with inclusive education.

## Housing and environment

**British Institute for Learning Disabilities**
Wolverhampton Road, Kidderminster, Worcestershire DY10 3PP
Tel: 01562 850251
Email: bild@bild.demon.co.uk
Website: www.bild.org.uk
Aims to improve the quality of life of all people with learning difficulties.

**Derbyshire Centre for Independent Living**
DCIL, Park Road, Ripley, Derbyshire DE5 3EF
Tel: 01773 740246
Aims to provide support to enable independent living.

**MENCAP (Royal Society for Mentally Handicapped Children and Adults)**
123 Golden Lane, London EC1Y ORT
Tel: 020 7454 0454
Email: information@mcncap.org.uk
Website: www.mencap.org.uk
Major organization for parents of children and adults with learning difficulties, with many local affiliated branches.

**National Housing Federation**
Lion Court, 25 Procter Street, London WC1V 6NY
Tel: 020 7067 1010
A national body for housing associations throughout the UK.

**Royal National Institute of Blind People**
105 Judd Street, London WC1H 9NE
Tel: 020 7388 1266
Runs schools and educational advisory services, colleges, courses, publications, aids and equipment.

**Royal National Institute for Deaf People**
19–23 Featherstone Street, London EC1Y 8SL
Tel: 020 7296 8000

**Sense**
101 Pentonville Road, London N1 9LG
Tel: 0845 127 0060
Text: 0845 127 0062
Email: info@sense.org.uk
Offers a wide range of services for parents of children who have dual sensory impairment including educational advice, training, information, support and advice.

**Sense Cymru**
Sense Cymru, Tŷ Penderyn, 26 High St, Merthyr Tydfil CF47 8DP
Sense Cymru, Tŷ Penderyn, 26 Stryd Fawr, Merthyr Tudful CF47 8DP
Ffôn/tel: 0845 127 0090
Ttestun/text: 0845 127 0092
Fffacs/fax: 0845 127 0091
Ebost/email: cymruenquiries@sense.org.uk

**Sense Northern Ireland**
Sense Family Centre, The Manor House, 51 Mallusk Road, Mallusk, County Antrim BT36 4RU
Tel: 028 9083 3430
Textphone: 028 9083 3430
Fax: 028 9084 4232
Email: nienquiries@sense.org.uk

**Sense Scotland**
43 Middlesex Street, Kinning Park, Glasgow G41 1EE
Tel: 0141 429 0294
Textphone: 0141 418 7170
Fax: 0141 429 0295
Email: info@sensescotland.org.uk

**Shelter**
88 Old Street, London EC1 9HU
Tel: 0808 800 444
Website: www.shelter.org.uk
Provides support for people who have disabilities in addition to cerebral palsy.

## Pressure groups

### British Council of Disabled People (BCODP)
Litchurch Plaza, Litchurch Lane, Derby DE24 8AA
Tel: 01332 295551
Email: anastasia@bcodp.org.uk
An umbrella group for local and specific interest pressure groups run by and for
people with disabilities.

### People First
F173 Riverside Business Park, Haldane Place, London SW18 4UQ
Tel: 0208 874 1377
Email: general@peoplefirstltd.com
Website: www.peoplefirstltd.com/index.php
A self-advocacy organization run by and for people with learning difficulties.

### RADAR
12 City Forum, 250 City Road, London ECIV 8AF
Tel: 020 7250 0212
Website: www.radar.org.uk
Promotes legislation, regulation and good practice and provides information
on matters affecting the lives of people with disabilities. Also assists disability
organizations to become more effective in their work.

## Disability arts forums

**Arcadea** (previously Northern Disability Arts Forum – NorDAF
Mea House, Ellison Place, Newcastle upon Tyne NE1 8XS
Tel: 0191 222 0708
Email: info@arcadea.org

### Arts and Disability Forum (Northern Ireland)
Ground Floor, 109–113 Royal Avenue, Belfast BT1 1FF
Tel: 028 9023 9450
Fax: 028 9024 7770
Textphone: 028 9032 5744
Email: info@adf.ie
Website: www.adf.ie

### British Wheel Sports Foundation
Guttmann Road, Stoke Mandeville, Buckinghamshire HP21 9PP
Tel: 01296 395995
Email: wheelpower@dial.pipex.com
Website: www.britishwheelchairsports.org
Provides training and development facilities for wheelchair users wishing to participate in sports activities.

### Calibre Audio Library
Aylesbury, Buckinghamshire HP22 5XQ
Tel: 01296 432339
Email: enquiries@calibre.org.uk
Website: www.calibre.org.uk
Has a wide range of cassettes of children's books which members can order.

### Cerebral Palsy Sport
CP Sport England & Wales, 5 Heathcoat Building, Nottingham Science Park, University Boulevard, Nottingham NG7 2QJ
Tel: 0115 925 7027
Fax: 0115 922 4666
Email: info@cpsport.org
Website: www.cpsport.org
Coordinating body for sport development and competition for people with cerebral palsy.

### DaDa South (Disability Arts Development Agency)
Office Suite G14, Springfield House, Maidstone, Kent ME14 2LP
Tel: 01622 685694
Emal: info@dada-south.org.uk

### DASh (Disability Arts Shropshire)
The Lantern, Meadow Farm Drive, Shrewsbury, Shropshire SY1 4NG
Tel: 01743 210840
Fax: 01743 466584
Textphone: 07800 746227
Email: mike@dasharts.org
Website: www.dasharts.org

### Disability Arts Cymru
Sbectrwm, Bwlch Road, Fairwater, Cardiff CF5 3EF
Telephone and textphone: 02920 551040
Email: post@dacymru.com
Website: www.dacymru.com

**Drake Music Project**
Drake Music, Rich Mix, 35–47 Bethnal Green Road, London E1 6LA
Tel: 020 7739 5444
Fax: 020 7729 8942
Email: info@drakemusicproject.org
Website: www.drakemusicproject.org
Enables disabled children and adults who are unable to play conventional musical instruments to compose and perform their own music.

**Edward Lear Foundation (Disability Arts Think-tank)**
Email: info@learfoundation.org.uk
Website: www.learfoundation.org.uk

**Kaleido**
Bradninch Place, Gandy Street, Exeter EX4 3LS
Tel: 01392 219440
Fax: 01392 219441
Email: info@kaleidoarts.org
Website: www.kaleidoarts.org

**Listening Books**
12 Lant Street, London SE1 1QH
Tel: 020 7407 9417
Email: info@listening-books.org.uk
Website: www.listening-books.org.uk
Offers a postal audio book service.

**North West Disability Arts Forum (NWDAF)**
MPAC Building, 1–27 Bridport House, Liverpool L3 5QF
Tel: 0151 707 1733
Fax: 0151 708 9355
Textphone: 0151 706 0365
Email: nwdaf@nwdaf.co.uk
Website: www.nwdaf.co.uk

**Riding for the Disabled Association (RDA)**
Norfolk House, 1a Tournament Court, Edgehill Drive, Warwick CV34 6LG
Tel: 0845 658 1082
Fax: 0845 658 1083
Website: www.riding-for-disabled.org.uk
RDA has local riding and carriage driving groups for people with disabilities.

# INTERNATIONAL ORGANIZATIONS BY COUNTRY

## AUSTRALIA

### Anne McDonald Centre
538 Dandenong Road, Caulfield, VIC 3162, Australia
Tel: (61 3) 9509 6324
Fax: (61 3) 9509 6321
Email: dealcc@vicnet.net.au
Website: www.annemcdonaldcentre.org.au/

### Australian Music Therapy Association (AMTA)
MBE 148/45 Glenferrie Road, Malvern VIC 3144, Australia
Tel: 03 9525 9625
Fax: 03 9507 2316
Website: www.austmta.org.au/

### Centre for Cerebral Palsy
PO Box 61, Mount Lawley, WA 6929, Australia
Tel: (08) 9443 0211
Toll free: 1800 198 263 (Australia only)
Fax: (08) 9444 7299
Email: info@tccp.com.au
Website: www.tccp.com.au

### Cerebral Palsy Australia
Suzanne Hawes, Scope, PO Box 608, Box Hill, VIC 3182, Australia
Tel: (61 3) 9843 2081
Fax: (61 3) 9899 2030
Email: shawes@scopevic.org.au

### Cerebral Palsy Education Centre Inc. (CPEC)
End of Beacon Street, Glen Waverley, Victoria 3150
PO Box 211, Glen Waverley, Victoria 3150
Tel: 03 9560 0700
Fax: 03 9560 0669
Email: info@cpec.org.au

### Conductive Education Centre of Western Australia
PO Box 1046, Scarborough WA 6922
Tel: 08 9361 7500
Website: www.conductiveedwa.com.au

## OPTIONS
PO Box 568, Kallangur, QLD 4503, Australia
Tel: (07) 3285 5522
Fax: (07) 3285 5522
Email: optionsctc@iprimus.com.au
Website: www.optionsctc.com.au

## BELGIUM
**Ligue d'aide aux infirmes moteurs cérébraux de
la communauté Française de Belgique**
1 rue Stanley, 69–71, Bruxelles, 1180, Belgium
Tel: 02 343 91 05

## CANADA
**ISAAC International Office**
49 The Donway West, Suite 308, Toronto, ON, M3C 3M9, Canada
Tel: +1 416 385 0351
Fax: +1 416 385 0352
Email: info@isaac-online.org

## FINLAND
**International Cerebral Palsy Society**
c/o Suomen CP-liitto, Malmin kauppatie 26, 00700 Helsinki, Finland
Tel: +358 400 421652
Email: aimo.stromberg@cp-liitto.fi
Website: www.icps.org.uk

## FRANCE
**Association des Paralyses de France (APF)**
17 boulevard Auguste-Blanqui, 17013 Paris, France
Ecoute Handicap Moteur: 0800 500 487
Ecoute SEP : 0800 854 976

## HUNGARY
**Peto Institute - Conductive Education**
Kútvölgyi út 6, Budapest, Hungary H-1125
Email: ce@peto.hu
Website: www.peto.hu/en

# INDIA

**Indian Institute of Cerebral Palsy**
P-35/1 Taratolla Road, Kolkata 700088, India
Tel: +91 33 2401 3488
Fax: +91 33 2401 4177
Email: info@iicpindia.com
Website: www.iicpindia.com

**Spastics Society of India**
K.C. Marg, Reclamation, Bandra West, Mumbai 400050, India

**Spastics Society of India**
Sion-Trombay Road, Chembur, Mumbai 400071, India

**Spastics Society of Karnataka**
No 31, 5th Cross, Off 5th Main, Indira Nagar, Bangalore – PIN: 560 038
Tel: 91 - 080 - 4074 5900 (100 lines)
Fax: +91 - 080 - 4074 5903

**Spastics Society of India**
St John's United Services Club, Opp. Afghan Church, Colaba, Mumbai 400005,
India
Tel: +91 (022) 215 0555 / 218 6813

# IRELAND

**Arts and Disability Ireland**
4th Floor, Sean O'Casey Centre, St. Mary's Road North, East Wall, Dublin 3
Republic of Ireland
Email: info@adiarts.ie
Tel: + 353 (0)1 8509 002
Fax:  + 353 (0)1 8509 037
Website: www.adiarts.ie

# ITALY

**Associazione Bambini Cerebrolesi – Lombardia**
Via Borgogna 5, Milan, Italy
Tel: +39 2 314077

# LITHUANIA

**Lithuanian Cerebral Palsy Association**
Strazdelio 1, 2600 Vilnius, Lithuania
Tel: 370 2 622466
Email: raffles@axion.net

## MEXICO
**APAC (Association pro Personas con P. Cerebral: Association for People with CP in Mexico)**
Dr Arce 104, Col. Doctores, Mexico DF, MX 06720, Mexico

## NEW ZEALAND
**Plunket**
Level 3, 40 Mercer Street, Wellington 6011
Tel: 0800 933 922
Email: plunket@plunket.org.nz
Website: www.plunket.org.nz

## PAKISTAN
**Anwar Shah Trust for Cerebral Palsy and Paralysis**
16 Awaisia Society College Road Township, Lahore, Pakistan
Tel (mobile): 0092 300 9400049
Tel: 0092 42 5118410, 8400751
Fax: 00 1 209 8855677
Email: info@cpfirst.org
Website: www.cpfirst.org

**Pakistan Society for the Rehabilitation of the Disabled**
111 Ferozepur Road, Lahore, Pakistan
Tel: +9242 3757 8253, +9242 3758 8681, +9242 3756 5580, +9242 3758 2860
Fax: +9242 3757 4936
Email: psrd@brain.net.pk
Website: www.psrd.org.pk

## SERBIA
**Cerebral Palsy Association of Serbia**
Panciceva 16, 11 000 Belgrade, Serbia

## SINGAPORE
**Spastic Children's Association of Singapore**
Cerebral Palsy Centre, 65 Pasir Ris Drive 1, Singapore 519529
Tel: (65) 6585-5600
Fax: (65) 6585-5603
Email: spastic@pacific.net.sg
Website: www.spastic.org.sg

## SLOVENIA

**SONCEK (Cerebral Palsy Association of Slovenia)**
Rožanska ulica 2, 1000 Ljubljana, Slovenia
Tel: +386 1 231 1057, 231 1058
Fax: +386 1 231 1060
Email: zveza@soncek.org
Website: www.soncek.org

## SOUTH AFRICA

**Eastern Transvaal Cerebral Palsy Association**
PO Box 807, Springs, 1560, South Africa
Tel:.(+27) 11 818 2337
Fax:.(+27) 11 818 2338

**United Cerebral Palsy Association**
PO Box 293, Rosettenville, 2130, South Africa
Tel: (011) 435 0386/7/8/9
Fax: (011) 435 3967
Email: marie@ucpa.za.org

**Western Cape Cerebral Palsy Association**
Vereniging vir serebraal verlamdes, Box 4267, Cape Town 8000, South Africa
St Giles Centre, 71 Klipfontein Road, Rondebosch 7700, South Africa

## SPAIN

**ASPACE (Spanish Federation for People with Cerebral Palsy)**
c./ General Zabala 29, Madrid 28002, Spain
Website: www.aspace.org

## USA

**American Association for Homecare**
2011 Crystal Drive, Suite 725, Arlington, Virginia 22202
Tel: (p) 703 836 6263  (f) 703 836 6730
Email: info@aahomecare.org
Website: www.aahomecare.org/

**American Association of People with Disabilities**
1629 K Street NW, Suite 950, Washington, DC 20006, USA
Tel: 202 457 0046 (V/TTY)
Toll free: 800 840 8844 (V/TTY)
Fax: 202 457 0473
Website: www.disabilityresources.org
Provides disability resources on the internet.

**American Music Therapy Association (AMTA)**
8455 Colesville Road, Suite 1000, Silver Spring, MD 20910
Tel: 301 589 3300
Fax: 301 589 5175
Website: www.musictherapy.org/

**Association of Waldorf School of North America**
Leader of Association Administration
Frances Kane, 2344 Nicollet Ave S., Minneapolis, MN 55404
Tel: 612 870 8310
Fax: 612 870 8316
Email: fkane@awsna.org

**Augmentative and Alternative Communication (AAC)**
**Connecting Young Kids (YAACK)**
Website: www.aac.unl.edu/yaack/index.html
Comprehensive website about Augmentative and Alternative Communication.

**4MYCHILD**
39555 Orchard Hill Place, Suite 365, Novi, MI 48375, USA
Tel: 1 800 4MYCHILD (1 800 469 2445)
Email: contactus@4mychild.com
Website: www.inclusioninstitutes.org
Organization supporting inclusion and communication.

**Home Health Pavilion Inc. (Jay seating system)**
5027 Route 9W, Newburgh, NY 12550
Tel: (866) 563 6812
Fax: (845) 569 1291
Email: sales@homehealthpavilion.com
Website: www.homehealthpavilion.com/jay-cushions-fit-adjustable-contour-seating-system

**Inter-American Conductive Education Association**
PO Box 3169, Toms River, NJ 08756-3169, USA
Toll free: (800) 824 2232 or (732) 797 2S66 (USA only)
Fax: (732) 797-2599
Website: www.iacea.org

**MOVE International**
1300 17th Street, City Centre, Bakersfield, CA 93301-4533, USA
Tel: 800 397 MOVE(6683)
Email: move-international@kern.org
Website: www.move-international.org

**National Disability Rights Network**
900 Second Street, NE, Suite 211, Washington, DC 20002, USA
Tel: 202 408 9514
Fax: 202 408 9520
TTY: 202 408 9521
Email: info@ndrn.org
Website feedback: webmaster@ndrn.org
Website: www.augcomm.com
Supplies information on a number of communication aid centres in the USA.

**NDTA**
1540 S. Coast Highway Ste 203, Laguna Beach, CA 92651
Tel: 800 869 9295
Fax: 949 376 3456
Email: info@ndta.org
Website: www.ndta.org/

**Rifton Equipment**
PO Box 260, Rifton, NY 12471-0260
Tel: 800 571 8198
Email: sales@rifton.com

**United Cerebral Palsy**
1825 K Street, NW Suite 600, Washington, DC 20006
Tel: (800) 872 5827, (202) 776 0406
Fax: (202) 776 0414
Email: info@ucp.org
Website: www.ucp.org

# REFERENCES

Acton.Shapiro and Contact a Family (2004) *No Time for Us: Relationships between Parents who have a Disabled Child. A Survey of over 2000 Parents in the UK.* London: Contact a Family.

Alderson, P. and Goodey, C. (1998) 'Doctors, ethics and special education.' *Journal of Medical Ethics 24,* 49–55.

Bax, M., Goldstein, M., Rosenbaum, P., Leviton, A. and Paneth, N. (2005) 'Proposed Definition and Classification of Cerebral Palsy.' *Developmental Medicine & Child Neurology,* 47, 571-576.

Black, L. (2001) *Lucy's Story: Autism and Other Adventures.* London: Jessica Kingsley Publishers.

Blair, E. and Stanley, F. (2007) 'Intrapartum asphyxia: A rare cause of cerebral palsy.' *Journal of Pediatrics 112,* 4, 515–519.

Clark, S.L. and Hankins, G.D. (2003) 'Temporal and demographic trends in cerebral palsy – fact and fiction.' *American Journal of Obstetrics and Gynecology 188,* 3, 628–633.

Collet, J.P., Vanasse, M., Marois, P., Amar, M., Goldberg, J., Lambert, J., *et al.* (2001) 'Hyperbaric oxygen for children with cerebral palsy: A randomized multicentre trial.' *The Lancet 357,* 582–586.

Colver, A. (2010) 'Why are children with cerebral palsy more likely to have emotional and behavioural difficulties?' *Developmental Medicine & Child Neurology,* 52, 980-987.

Crossley, R. (1994) *Facilitated Communication Training.* New York: Teachers College Press.

Crossley, R. (2000) *Speechless: Facilitating Communication for People without Voices.* New York: Teachers College Press.

Crothers, B. and Payne, R.S. (1959) *The Natural History of Cerebral Palsy.* Cambridge: Harvard University Press.

Day, S.M., Wu, Y.W., Strauss, D.J. and Shavelle, R.M. (2004) 'Prognosis for Ambulation in Cerebral Palsy: A Population-Based Study.' *Pediatrics,* 114, 5, 1264-1271.

Doman, G.J. (1991) *What to do About Your Brain.* Pennsylvania State University: M. Evans.

Einarsdottir, K., Vik, T., Gudmundsson, H.R.S., Eiriksdottir, A., Indredavik, M.S. and Sigurdardottir, S. (2010) 'Behavioural and emotional symptoms of preschool children with cerebral palsy: a population-based study.' *Developmental Medicine & Child Neurology,* 52, 1056-1061.

Erickson, K.A. (2000) 'All children are ready to learn: An emergent versus readiness perspective in early literacy assessment.' *Seminars in Speech and Language 21,* 3, 193–203.

Finnie, N.R. (1997) *Handling the Young Child with Cerebral Palsy at Home.* 3rd edn. Oxford: Butterworth-Heinemann.

Fry, E. (1986) *An Equal Chance for Disabled People? A Study of Discrimination in Employment.* The Spastics Society, available at: http://research.dwp.gov.uk/asd/asd5/ihr/ih031.pdf, accessed 1 February 2012.

Fuchs, D., Compton, D.L., Fuchs, L.S., Bouton, B. and Caffrey, E. (2011) 'The construct and predictive validity of a dynamic assessment of young children learning to read: Implications for RTI frameworks.' *Journal of Learning Disabilities 44,* 4, 339–347.

Glennen, S. and DeCoste, D.C. (1997) *The Handbook of Augmentative and Alternative Communication.* San Diego, CA: Singular.

Head, T. (n.d.) *Forced Sterilization in the United States: A Short History.* Available at http://civilliberty.about.com/od/gendersexuality/tp/Forced-Sterilization-History.htm, accessed 17 December 2011.

Hebb, D.O. (1949) *The Organization of Behavior: A Neuropsychological Theory.* New York: Wiley.

Humphrey, A. (2006) 'Children behaving badly: A case of misunderstanding?' *The Psychologist 19*, 8, 494–495.

Ito, J., Araki, A., Tanaka, H., Tasaki, T. and Cho, K. (1997) 'Intellectual status of children with cerebral palsy after elementary education.' *Pediatric Rehabilitation 1*, 4, 199–206.

Johnson, A. (2002) 'Prevalence and characteristics of children with cerebral palsy.' *Europe Developmental Medicine and Child Neurology 44*, 9, 633–640.

Joseph, R. (2000) 'The Basal Ganglia.' In R. Joseph, *Neuropsychiatry, Neuropsychology, Clinical Neuroscience*, 3rd edn. New York: Academic Press. Available at www.brainmind.com/BasalGanglia.html, accessed 31 December 2009.

Kaufman, M., Silverberg, C. and Odette, F. (2003) *The Ultimate Guide to Sex and Disability: For All of Us Who Live with Disabilities, Chronic Pain and Illness.* San Fransisco: Cleis Press.

Kondo, K. (2000) 'Congenital Minamata Disease: Warnings from Japan's experience.' *Journal of Child Neurology 15*, 458–464.

Koziol, L.F. and Budding, D.E. (2009) *Subcortical Structures and Cognition: Implications for Neuropsychological Assessment.* New York: Springer.

Lantolf, J.P. and Poehner, M.E. (2011) 'Dynamic assessment in the classroom: Vygotskian praxis for second language development.' *Language Teaching Research 15*, 1, 11–33.

Lawless, J. (2002) *Encyclopaedia of Essential Oils: The complete guide to the use of aromatic oils in aromatherapy, herbalism, health and well-being.* London: Thorsons.

Levitt, S. (1977) *Treatment of Cerebral Palsy and Motor Delay.* Oxford: Blackwell Scientific.

Liu, J.M., Li, S., Lin, Q. and Li, Z. (1999) 'Prevalence of cerebral palsy in China.' *International Journal of Epidemiology 28*, 949–954.

MemoryZine (2010) 'Introduction to Neuroplasticity.' Available at www.memoryzine.com/neuroplasticity.htm, accessed 11 November 2011.

Minear, W.L. (1956) 'A classification of cerebral palsy.' *Pediatrics 18*, 841–852.

Musselwhite, C. (2010) *Augmentative/Alternative Communication Intervention.* Available at www.aacintervention.com, accessed 1 January 2010.

National Child Traumatic Stress Network, National Center for Child Traumatic Stress, 11150 Olympic Blvd. Suite 770, Los Angeles, CA 90064. Available at www.nctsn.org, accessed 11 November 2011.

Nelson, K.B. and Ellenberg, J.H. (1982) 'Children who "outgrew" cerebral palsy.' *Pediatrics 69*, 5, 529–536.

O'Brien, C.L. and O'Brien, J. (2000) *The Origins of Person-Centered Planning: A Community of Practice Perspective.* Available at www.thechp.syr.edu//PCP_History.pdf, accessed 9 August 2009.

Oelwein, P.L. (1995) *Teaching Reading to Children with Down Syndrome: A Guide for Parents and Teachers.* Bethesda, MD: Woodbine House.

Origins of Cerebral Palsy (n.d.) 'Forms of Cerebral Palsy.' Available at www.originsofcerebralpalsy.com/02-index-forms.html, accessed 30 December 2009.

Osler, W. and Baird, H.W. (1991) *Cerebral Palsies of Children: A Clinical Study from the Infirmary for Nervous Diseases, Philadelphia.* London: MacKeith.

Phelps, W.M. (1948) 'Characteristic psychological variations in cerebral palsy.' *The Nervous Child 7*, 1, 10–13.

Rea-Dickins, P. and Poehner, M.E. (2011) 'Addressing issues of access and fairness in education through dynamic assessment.' *Assessment in Education: Principles, Policy and Practice 18*, 2, 95–97.

Robertson, C.M.T., Watt, M-J. and Yasui, Y. (2007) 'Changes in the prevalence of cerebral palsy for children born very prematurely within a population-based program over 30 years.' *Journal of the American Medical Association 297*, 24, 2733–2740.

Romski, M.A. and Sevcik, R.A. (1993) 'Language Learning through Augmented Means: The Process and its Products.' In S.F. Warren and J. Reichle (eds) *Enhancing Children's Communication*, Volume 2. Baltimore, MD: Paul H. Brookes.

Rong-zhi, W. (1996) 'An approach to treatment of cerebral palsy of children by foot massage: A clinical analysis of 132 cases.' *1996 Beijing International Reflexology Conference (Report)*. Beijing: China Preventive Medical Association and the Chinese Society of Reflexology.

Rosenbaum, P., Barnitt, R. and Brand, H.L. (1975) 'The Consequence of Impaired Movement: A Hypothesis and Review.' In K.S. Holt (ed.) *Movement and Child Development*. London: Heinemann.

Sandberg, A.D. (2006) 'Reading and spelling abilities in children with severe speech impairments and cerebral palsy at 6, 9, and 12 years of age in relation to cognitive development: A longitudinal study.' *Developmental Medicine and Child Neurology 48*, 8, 629–634.

Schaefer, G.B. (2008) 'Genetics considerations in cerebral palsy.' *Seminars in Pediatric Neurology 15*, 1, 21–26.

Schmidt, P.J. and Vojens, D.K. (2003) *A Modernized Approach Suggests a New Definition of Cerebral Palsy: Now is the Time for a Paradigm Shift*. Frederiksberg, Denmark: Danish Society for Cerebral Palsy. In 'New CO. Ce3rebral Palsy – Hold to the light' available as PDF at: http://livingwithcerebralpalsy.com/pdfs/cpuk.pdf, accessed 31 January 2012.

Sheridan, M.D. (1975) *Children's Developmental Progress from Birth to Five Years*. Windsor: NFER Publishing.

Sinha, G., Corry, P., Subesinghe, D., Wild, J. and Levene, M.I. (1997) 'Prevalence and type of cerebral palsy in a British ethnic community: The role of consanguinity.' *Developmental Medicine and Child Neurology 39*, 4, 259–262.

Stanton, M. (2006) *Communication and Learning Enterprises*. Available at www.contactcandle.co.uk/files/guidelines_for_the_provision_of_motor_planning_training_version_2_1.pdf, accessed 31 January 2012.

Sullivan, P.B., Juszczak, E., Bachlet, A.M.E., Lambert, B. *et al.* (2005) 'Gastrostomy tube feeding in children with cerebral palsy: A prospective, longitudinal study.' *Developmental Medicine and Child Neurology 47*, 2, 77–85.

Turner, B.M., Paradiso, S., Marvel, C.L., Pierson, R., *et al.* (2007) 'The cerebellum and emotional experience.' *Neuropsychologia 45*, 6, 1331–1341.

UN Convention on the Rights of the Child, 1989 United Nations, Treaty Series, vol. 1577, p. 3, available at: www.unhcr.org/refworld/docid/3ae6b38f0.html, accessed 17 December 2011.

Wichers, M.J., van der Schouw, Y.T., Moons, K.G., Stam, H.J. and van Nieuwenhuizen, O. (2001) 'Prevalence of cerebral palsy in The Netherlands (1977–1988).' *European Journal of Epidemiology 17*, 6, 527–532.

Winter, S., Autry, A., Boyle, C. and Yeargin-Allsopp, M. (2002) 'Trends in the prevalence of cerebral palsy in a population-based study.' *Pediatrics 110*, 6, 1220–1225.

Worwood, V. (1991) *The Complete Book of Essential Oils and Aromatherapy: Over 600 Natural, Non-Toxic and Fragrant Recipes to Create Health, Beauty and a Safe Home*. Novato, CA: New World Library.

# ABOUT THE AUTHOR

**Marion Stanton** is a special needs teacher and Augmentative and Alternative Communication (AAC) practitioner. She is the mother of three children, including Dan, who has cerebral palsy. She has previously worked in nursing, occupational therapy and housing. Since becoming a parent of a child with a disability, Marion has co-founded a parent-run early learning group for children with disabilities (PALACE) and has been an active member of the Alliance for Inclusive Education, which campaigns for the right of all children and young people with disabilities to be educated in the mainstream. She has also been involved in conferences on communication and access for children with disabilities. She is currently lead assessor and trainer for Communication and Learning Enterprises Limited (CandLE). This is a not-for-profit organization working with people with communication difficulties in a number of ways, including training teachers who are able to include pupils with disabilities in mainstream schools, producing resources for communication aid users, helping people to choose communication devices to suit their needs, and helping special and mainstream schools to use AAC to support literacy and learning.

# INDEX